What Others Are Saying About T[...]

Effortlessly readable, immensely informative, *The Secretary's Friend* is a memorable book. —WYOU TV

Anne Morton's book is a quality, superior work. —Midwest Book Review

An EXCELLENT book. —Virginia Gaustad, Professor of Office Automation, Crafton Hills College

The Secretary's Friend offers expert advice to *today's* secretary who has ambitions to advance to management positions. This readable and handy reference tool is written for the automated office of the 80's. —Ottowa (Canada) Citizen

The Secretary's Friend is a useful, easy-to-read handbook. —(Educator's) Curriculum Product Review

An excellent resource publication for every office. —Senator John W. Warner

A highly recommended and valuable reference source for all office professionals. . .an excellent book for administrative support personnel. —National Business Education Association, Anne L. Matthews, President

Anne Morton's book provides good advice and timely insights for those in the secretarial profession. —Charles S. Robb, Governor of Virginia

The Secretary's Friend should be read by all secretaries and by the persons who employ them. —Washington Business School, Albert P. Coppola, President

I recommend *The Secretary's Friend* to anyone who works in an office. —Congressman Philip M. Crane

The Secretary's Friend is the office manual that not only helps the secretary meet high standards of performance but can serve as a reference tool for everyone else in the office. —Mary Wine, Association of Independent Colleges and Schools

Anne Morton has brought together an impressive amount of practical information that is invaluable to the professional secretary in any setting. —Longwood College, Janet D. Greenwood, President

For working with people with confidence and effectiveness, this book is a must. —Fairfax County Public Schools, Robert R. Spillane, Superintendent

A superb resource for todays' secretary. The coverage of new office technology and how it is rapidly expanding the secretary's role is desperately needed—not only by secretaries but also by those who train tomorrow's work force. —Future Business Leaders Of America, Edward D. Miller, President/Chief Executive Officer

Anne Morton understands excellence and knows how to coach people interested in achieving it. She is indeed "The Secretary's Friend". —Illinois State Board of Education, Elam K. Hertzler, Executive Assistant/Chief of Staff

Secretaries have never had a better friend than Anne Morton, the intelligent author of *The Secretary's Friend*. Every secretary, everyone who inhabits or runs an office, should have such a friend. —Hampden-Sydney College, Josiah Bunting III, President

The Secretary's Friend

The Office Management Manual

The Secretary's Friend

The Office Management Manual

by Anne Morton

LOWEN PUBLISHING
TORRANCE, CALIFORNIA 90504-0870

Lowen Publishing
Post Office Box 6870-130
Torrance, California 90504-0870

Library of Congress Cataloging in Publication Data:

Morton, Anne M. (Frances Anne Murphy)
The Secretary's Friend

Bibliography: Includes Index
1. Management—Office
2. Secretarial

1. Title

LC 86-45541
ISBN No. 0-933051-16-6-Hard Cover
ISBN No. 0-933051-33-6-Soft Cover

This book, published by Lowen Publishing, is available at special discounts for bulk purchases for premiums, sales promotions, fund-raising, or educational use. Book excerpts or special editions can also be created to specification. Contact Lowen Publishing at the address above.

10 9 8 7 6 5 4 3 2

Printed in the United States of America

Dedication

To my beloved and late husband Buck, the light of my life for twenty-seven years, whose loving memory was my inspiration, encouragement, and strength to write this book; and to my son Chip who gave me special encouragement and support when I needed it the most.

THE SECRETARY'S FRIEND

Acknowledgments

Words are inadequate to express my deep gratitude to the one at the top of this list—my dear friend and neighbor, Carla Schardt. Her many hours of proofing, editing, and suggesting ideas contributed to the final outcome of this book. But most of all, Carla, thank you for your love and unending moral support at a difficult time in both of our lives.

Kelan Putbrese, a talented artist and former student, who designed the logo for the Secretary's Friend and book.

In addition, the following friends contributed time, effort, and ideas to my book: Anne M. Rowe, Barbara Lovenvirth, David Hunsaker, Keith E. Putbrese, Virginia Russell, and Carl E. Jorgensen.

Disclaimer

This book is designed to provide information in regard to the subject matter covered. It is sold with the understanding that the publisher and author are not engaged in rendering legal, accounting or other professional services. If such expert assistance is required, the services of a competent professional should be sought.

It is not the purpose of this book to reprint all the information that is otherwise available to the author and/or publisher but to compliment, amplify and supplement other texts. For more information, see the many references in the Appendix or consult appropriate library resources.

Every effort has been made to make this manual as complete and as accurate as possible. However THERE MAY BE MISTAKES both typographical and in content. Therefore this text should be used only as a general guide and not as the ultimate source for information about the secretarial sciences and/or allied areas of expertise. Furthermore, this manual contains information on such areas only up to the printing date.

The purpose of this book is to educate and entertain. The author and Lowen Publishing shall have neither liability nor responsibility to any person or entity with respect to any loss or damage caused or alleged to be caused directly or indirectly by the information contained in this book.

NOTE

In the interest of avoiding awkward sentence structure, the male pronoun is used throughout the book; it should be understood that this implies both sexes.

About the Author

Anne Morton currently heads the business education department at Langley High School, McLean, Virginia. She is a native Virginian, received her B.S. degree at Longwood College in Virginia and did her graduate work at Columbia University in New York City.

The author, a veteran of thirty years teaching in business education with specialties in typewriting, shorthand, word processing, and office technology, has trained thousands of secretaries. She has also helped to develop teaching curricula which are being used at the national level. Morton's articles on business education and modern office technologies have appeared in national publications, and she has lectured to other teachers and secretaries at local, state, and national seminars and conferences.

In addition, to the author's devotion to teaching and the secretarial profession, she is active in community, educational, and civic affairs. Morton is the vice-president of the McLean Business and Professional Association; she is also a member of the Corporate Foundations Board for Hampden-Sidney College, the National Press Club, the Fairfax County School Superintendent's Business/Industry Advisory Council, and a Board member of the Congressional Award for Virginia's 10th District.

Besides teaching, Morton owns two office supply stores in the Washington, DC area and is the publisher of an internationally distributed newsletter for secretaries, *THE SECRETARY'S FRIEND,* which is distributed through other office supply dealers. *THE SECRETARY'S FRIEND* is a member/sponsor of The National Task Force for the Image of the Secretary.

The author was the 1985 Virginia Business Teacher of the Year and listed in the March 1986 edition of ''Washington Woman'' as one of 50 outstanding Washington Women for achievement and commitment.

Anne Morton is the widow of Claiborne B. Morton, Jr. and has one son, Claiborne B. Morton III, currently serving in the United States Air Force.

Table of Contents

Preface

PART I INTRODUCTION 21

Chapter 1 **The Changing Role of the Secretary** 23
Attitudes Are Changing, Too 24
Are You Ready for a Name Change? 25

Chapter 2 **Your First Job as a Secretary** 27

PART II THE SECRETARY MANAGES 31

Chapter 3 **The Office Space and Equipment** 33
The Secretary's Role in Office Design Planning 33
Is Your Work Space Sufficient? 34
The Economics of Ergonomics 36
Place Video Terminals in the Right Light for Sight 37
Get the Most Mileage Out of Your Copier 38
Another Time—A Different File 40
Micrographics—Another Secretarial Friend 43
Spring Cleaning—Once a Month for Desk Efficiency 43
Office Relocation Can be Easier 45

Chapter 4

The Office as a Community 49
Super Supervisor 49
Decisions, Decisions, Decisions 50
Is Flexitime, Job Sharing, or Telecommuting for You? 52
Office Ethics—How Much is Enough? 54
Keeping Information Confidential 55
The Secretary Can Help Keep Computer Secrets 56
The Coffee Break—Food for Thought 57
When the Holiday Syndrome Hits the Office 58
Does the Hat Get Passed Too Often? 60

Chapter 5

The Office as a Production Unit 61
Productivity—A Buzz Word That Will Last 61
Procedures Manuals Save Time and Increase Production 61
Logging Work Increases Productivity 63
The Secretary's Role in Planning and Attending Meetings 63
Meeting Types 64
Preparation Can Make the Difference 65
Making Meetings Worthwhile 66
Taking Minutes at the Meeting 67
Follow-up—The Real Difference 69
The Secretary's Role in Planning a Convention 69
Teleconferencing vs. Traditional Meetings 73
IRS Time—The Secretary Helps Get Ready 74
Planning the Business Trip 76
Absence of the Boss 78
A Plan for Handling Office Mail 80
Handling Mail the Electronic Way 82
Cost-Cutting Correspondence 85

PART III THE SECRETARY COMMUNICATES 87

Chapter 6

Keeping the Lines of Communication Open 89
Open Communication — Lifeblood of the Office 89
The Secretary Listens 90

Chapter 7

And the Word was Written 93
The Secretary Writes 93
The Secretary Answers Routine Correspondence 94
Handwriting in the Modern Office—YOU BET! 97

Shorthand Rusty? Brush Up 97
Perplexed About Paragraphs? 100
Which Salutations? 101
Now Which Closing for the Letter? 102
How to Eliminate Sex Bias in Writing 103
Use an Economic Format 104
Processing Business Reports 107
Preparing Financial Reports 110
Good Proofreading Improves Productivity 111

Chapter 8 **And the Word was Spoken** **113**
The Secretary Speaks 113
An Effective Conversationalist 113
Techniques in Speech Presentation 114
The Telephone—An Important Business Tool 116
Telephone Personality—Create It 116
The Secretary Dictates 120

PART IV THE SECRETARY HANDLES PEOPLE 123

Chapter 9 **The Outside World** **125**
Secretary—The Good-will Ambassador 125
The Secretary Greets the Office Visitor 125
When Appointments Run Behind: Wall-to-Wall Visitors 126
Public Relations Liaison for the Office 128
The Mechanics of Preparing Press Releases 130
From the Word Processor to the Camera 131
Handling Unscrupulous Callers 133

Chapter 10 **Within the Office Environment** **137**
Secretaries—The Human Factor in the Office System 137
The Role of Staff Confidante 139
Secretary and Boss—A Winning Team 141
Adjusting to a New Boss 142
Stress—Learning to Cope 143
Criticism—You Can Handle It 145
The Negative Approach Isn't All Bad 146
Office Politics—It Does Exist 147
Executive "Suite-Talk" 148
When Illness Hits Your Office 149
The Secretary Deals with the Two-Martini Lunch Crowd 151
The Art of Delegating Authority 152
How to Ask for a Raise 153

PART V THE SECRETARY STAYS WELL INFORMED 157

Chapter 11

Information—Sources and Resources **159**
Professional Reading 159
Reference Sources for the Office 159
Suggestions to Improve Your Reading Speed 160
Newsletters—A Growing Pool of Information 161
Mailing Lists—Another Phenomenon 163
Special Direct Mail Terms 164
The U.S. Postal Service—A Cost-Effective Friend 166
Other Special Postal Terms 169
Metric. . .When? 172
Is Another Keyboard on the Horizon? 174
Professional Secretaries International (PSI) 176

Chapter 12

Quick and Easy Brush-up—Spelling, Punctuation, Grammar **179**
Spelling—The Sandtrap of the Secretary 179
- Words Frequently Misspelled 182
Punctuation and Mechanics 183
Punctuation 183
- A Dash (—) of Punctuation 185
- Hyphens—A Different Dash of Confusion 185
- That Big Little Apostrophe 187
Mechanics 189
- Getting It Together with Numbers 189
- To Shift or Not to Shift? 195
Grammatically Speaking 198
- Who or Whom? 198
- Which or That 199
- These and Those for This and That 199
- Each and Every 200
- Shall or Will? 200
- Misplaced or Dangling Modifiers 201
- Subjunctive Mood 201
- Possessive with the Gerund 202
- Position of Prepositions 202
- Active and Passive Voice 203
English Usage - Which Word and Why 204

Chapter 13 **Secretarial Tips and Timesavers** **209**

APPENDIX 215

A - BUSINESS "BABBLE"—Do Not Let It Intimidate YOU! **215**
Word Processing/Computer Glossary Acronyms 215

B - Abbreviations **223**
Most Commonly Used in Business 223
Abbreviations Used in Law 226
Abbreviations Used in Medicine 227
Medical Prefixes and Suffixes 228
State Abbreviations 229
Frequently Used Address Abbreviations 229
Geographic Locations 230

C - Commonly Used Foreign Words and Phrases **231**

D - Special Signs and Symbols **233**

E - Travel Tips for the Secretary on the Go **237**

F - Examples of Document Format **241**
Letter Styles 241
Interoffice Memorandums 245
Press Release 246

G - Secretarial References, Books and Manuals **247**

H - Proofreading Marks **250**

Index **251**

Updates/Success Catalog Coupon **253**

Order Form **256**

Preface

My early training as a secretary provided some of the most valuable experience I could possibly have had. I learned to work with people, which helped prepare me for the teaching profession. I went from one necessary and noble profession to another. Both have brought many rewards and much fulfillment, pleasure, satisfaction, and happiness into my life. Secretaries, particularly those I have taught as students, are very special to me.

As a business education teacher for the past thirty years, I have trained thousands of secretaries for business, industry, and local and federal government. Because of the interest expressed by former students, secretaries, business acquaintances, and secretarial training schools for *The Secretary's Friend,* the newsletter I write and distribute internationally, I developed this book. I hope that it is as well received as the newsletter.

Since my first secretarial job over three decades ago, the business office has undergone many changes. The old, blank, black keyboard on which I gave my first typing instruction has become a colorful electronic marvel with memory and editing functions. A new keyboard, the Dvorak, is on the horizon, and by the year 2000, it is predicted that secretaries will be able to talk to their typewriters via automatic voice recognition.

With computerization, business terminology has become highly technical. The carbon copy has been replaced by the courtesy copy done on a photocopier; metric measurements are used more and more by business and industry; and ten-key adding machines, once so scarce that teachers had to sign up for them to average grades, have been replaced by pocket electronic printing calculators—one in every student's pocket, executive briefcase and secretarial drawer. The two digit postal zones are now nine digits, and electronic mail systems send pictures, graphics and written documents all over the world in just hours. The standard, gray file cabinet has been replaced by color-coded lateral shelf files, microfiche, and other electronic records management systems. Even the telephone has acquired word processing capabilities and is casually used for low-cost communication throughout the world. Technological changes in procedures and equipment will inevitably continue. However, one element has not and will not change—the need for competent, well-qualified secretaries. Yours is, indeed, a necessary profession.

You may have heard that the future office will be paperless, that robots will replace you. IT WON'T HAPPEN. In fact, there is already a severe shortage of secretaries. The U.S. Labor Department has predicted that by 1990 there will be 5.25 million secretarial positions open nationwide—and rising by over 300,000 per year. True, in some large corporations, robots are already performing repetitive, labor-intensive office tasks such as delivering mail or taking paper back and forth to the copy room. Welcome them with open arms. Let them perform these time-consuming operations and thus allow you time to utilize skills which machines do not possess—skills recognized as those of a PROFESSIONAL secretary. In the pages ahead, *The Secretary's Friend* offers suggestions about new procedures and timesaving techniques that will help you fulfill your professional role. I hope that secretaries, secretarial students, managers, and others who work in a business office discover professional approaches to making routine jobs easier, less tedious, more cost effective, and perhaps even fun. I also hope you will find solutions to some of the problems we all face in handling people, new equipment, and new procedures in the office environment. Turn to this book as you would to a friend—**THE SECRETARY'S FRIEND.**

Part I

Introduction

CHAPTER 1

The Changing Role of the Secretary

We must have perseverance and, above all, confidence in ourselves. We must believe that we are gifted for something.

—Madame Curie

The modern office is being assailed by unprecedented technological changes. Outdated equipment is giving way to innovative machines, and old methods are being replaced by fresh approaches. What impact do these changes have on the role of the secretary? PLENTY. As an integral and vital part of the office evolution, the secretary has become the nerve center of business, industry and government at all levels.

Secretarial responsibilities have broadened to the point where the office may be called the secretary's private domain. Besides an enhanced image, the role of the secretary is changing. Secretaries are not only using word processors, but many are using computers for financial applications, spreadsheets and graphics. The secretary is now more often called an administrative assistant—a reflection of expanded responsibilities. New orientations are needed to meet the challenges and demands created by new technologies. Proficiency in a skill is not enough. You must also have the ability to transfer your skills from one technology to another. You need to be able to listen, to think, and to follow directions. Prerequisites for success in any job, these skills are especially vital in today's office environment.

Listening has never been more important. Since much data is processed from the spoken word, either in person or by electronic media, directions must first be understood in order to be followed.

A secretary must have the ability to make decisions, set priorities, and use good judgment. No machine, regardless of its sophistication, can offer GOOD JUDGMENT. With busy executives constantly on the go, more office decisions are being left to the secretary's discretion. The secretary must be willing and able to handle the pressures that come with increased responsibility.

Communication skills are also prerequisites for success in dealing with people, procedures, and machines. Good language skills are necessary in accurately transferring written and oral messages. Correct spelling, punctuation, and grammar are also important components in editing, proofreading and working with word processing equipment.

No longer isolated at one desk in one office with one boss, the modern secretary must be able to get along with large numbers of people. Since many are already sharing office space, equipment, and bosses, an understanding of the overall operation of the organization is essential if the secretary is to function as a good-will ambassador—the liaison between the supervisor and other staff members or between the boss and client. The secretary is the human factor in the office. I challenge the machine that can claim this role. Never underestimate the public relations impact that secretaries have.

Attitudes are Changing, Too

In addition to expanded responsibilities, automation has also created changes in job titles, promotion opportunities, and most important, management attitudes. Job hunters no longer spurn secretarial jobs as career choices but rather flock to them. Management now recognizes that advancing technology requires more proficiency and higher education; secretaries enjoy better and higher-paying job prospects. The secretary is a professional.

In the past, the career progress of the secretary was often linked to the manager's or executive's climb up the corporate ladder. Today, opportunities for advancement are independent of the executive's success. Now, as never before, secretaries get a chance to put their education, training, and job experience to good use. By doing so, the secretary reaps the benefits of professional recognition, enhanced managerial and supervisory opportunities, and speedier advancement in the corporate structure. Attitudes toward the secretary will continue to change as old myths fade and modern realities are accepted. Who knows where today's secretary may end up—the White House perhaps? Don't laugh. Young Lyndon Baines Johnson, 36th President of the United States, once worked as a secretary, not to mention Art Linkletter who supported himself as a clerk-typist while he was struggling to become an entertainer. Hang in there, Secretaries.

Are You Ready for a Name Change?

To keep up the contemporary pace, specialization of skills is necessary in many large organizations. Specialization has caused job title changes that more clearly describe the duties involved. This has also brought about a change in the names of some secretarial jobs.

The word "secretary" is derived from the Latin meaning "secret" or "one who is entrusted with secrets." The New College Edition of the American Heritage Dictionary defines a secretary as "A person employed to handle correspondence, keep files, and do clerical work for an individual or company."

There is little wonder, then, that with these definitions, a multitude of new titles has been assigned to the individual who has a mastery of office skills and is responsible for keeping the office running smoothly. Some of the more appropriate descriptions that have replaced the traditional title of secretary follow:

Administrative Assistant	Business Manager
Logistics Coordinator	Business Assistant
Office Administrator	Administrative Coordinator
Office Manager	Administrative Specialist
Office Coordinator	Administrative Executive
Regional Director	Office Services Coordinator
Executive Officer	Administrative Office Aide
Manager Assistant	Technical Assistant
Professional Assistant	Staff Assistant
Marketing Assistant	Staff Aide

New specialties—new names. Whatever your title, everyone knows that you are the one indispensable individual necessary to the survival of the office.

CHAPTER 2

Your First Job as a Secretary

Great is the art of beginning.
—Henry Wadsworth Longfellow

At some point, we all have to report to a first job. For some, this is harder than for others. Fear and anxiety make what should be a time of eager anticipation a time of tension. As you step out that first day and proceed through the first weeks and months, you should be self-confident. This is not an easy task at first, but remember someone had confidence in you or you would not have been hired in the first place.

Dressing in a manner appropriate to the office will make you feel businesslike and professional. Being friendly, courteous and helpful will gain the respect of your new boss and fellow employees. Smile a lot. As you begin to learn the ins and outs for your particular job, you will gain self-assurance, the mark of the true professional.

Here are a few suggestions to help make that first secretarial job go smoothly.

- Learn all you can as soon as possible about company policies. What are the rules on arrival and quitting times, lunch and coffee breaks, overtime, smoking, sick leave, and personal telephone calls? Begin by abiding by all regulations.
- Be sure you understand the management structure of your office. Will you report to and receive job assignments from one person or

several? If you are assigned to a word processing center, this is especially important since projects will originate from various departments.

- Learn as quickly as possible the names of all employees with whom you work. Be sure that you spell and pronounce their names correctly.

The will to succeed is important to anyone's career. Be determined to do your best. When facing new duties, make up your mind that you will master them. With this positive mind set, you will do exactly that.

Whether you are approaching your first job or a new job, consider these time-honored recommendations that apply to any situation:

- Listen carefully to all instructions. Ask questions if they are unclear. Effective listening is a business tool. USE it.
- Write down everything. Do not trust your memory—there are too many things to remember in the beginning.
- Concentrate on the assigned task. Do not think about the second job until you finish the first. There will be time enough to juggle several assignments after you have mastered each job.
- Strive for accuracy. Do not settle for less-than-perfect work. Repeat a task until you achieve your goal. Speed will come later.
- Do not rush. Allow plenty of time to do what is required. Rushing causes a high percentage of errors.
- Practice patience. Watch your emotions. A new job tries anyone's patience, and emotions may get out of hand.

The new secretary needs to develop habits that can be carried to future positions whether they be secretarial or management.

- Keep an up-to-date calendar of all office activities, including meeting dates, conventions, and vacation times for staff members.

Besides a daily calendar, maintain an appointment book for your employer.

- The use of a tickler or current action file will also keep you a step ahead of the job. A tickler file is a follow-up file where records are organized by date. Other names for such a file are ''pending'' or ''hold for action.'' A tickler file assures a smooth, punctual work flow within the office community.
- Maintain a reading file. In your spare time, refer to copies of documents and correspondence in the office file. You will gain perspective on your job and the company at large. Become familiar with terminology frequently used in dictation or in office conversations. Develop shorthand outlines for often-used terms.
- Develop proficient reading habits. The faster you read, the quicker you can do your job.
- Keep communication channels open by being clear and concise in all written and oral instructions.
- Try to simplify office procedures. As you adjust to your new job, constantly look for ways to save time. Efficient methods of completing routine secretarial jobs can keep them from becoming unpleasant drudgery. Keep abreast of the latest office supplies and equipment available on the market, and try to stay current about new computer software. These tools make your job easier.
- Learn how to do other people's tasks. You will become invaluable if you can pitch in when a fellow worker is sick or away on vacation.
- Volunteer for extra work. If a particular project requires extra hours, evenings or weekends, ask to be involved. Your initiative and commitment will not go unnoticed.
- Attend meetings and seminars relating to your profession. Discover more about Professional Secretaries International (PSI) and the local chapters near you.

Finally, take a positive psychological stance on that first job: (1) Face the fact that some duties are less attractive than others; (2) Take things in stride—do not let minor irritations get you down; (3) Ask yourself where you want to be in the next five years. Then ask yourself what you are doing to get there. YOUR FUTURE IS UP TO YOU AND IT BEGINS WITH THAT FIRST JOB. The doors of opportunity are marked "push."

Part II

The Secretary Manages

CHAPTER 3

The Office Space and Equipment

Productivity is a measure of not how hard we work, but of how well we use our intelligence, our imagination and our capital.

—Henry Ford II

The Secretary's Role in Office Design Planning

Once the traditional secretary was isolated in a small area with one boss, taking dictation, answering routine calls and correspondence, and manually filing documents. Today's secretary is in the unique position of being part of overall management. The office itself is a production unit whose components are space and equipment. Computer terminals, word processors, copiers, and other automated equipment have not only increased office efficiency and productivity, but have strengthened the role of the secretary to that of office SUPERSTAR.

With automation comes interaction of people with machines. Today the office copier has become as popular a gathering place as yesterday's old-fashioned water cooler. Portable microwave ovens and refrigerators, appearing in offices as desk bases and space fillers, compete with copy machines for floor space.

The relationship between equipment and users increasingly dictates that many secretaries—even those not acting as office managers—become closely involved in planning the office layout and selecting furniture and equipment. Smart secretaries set up a schedule for all office personnel to receive appropriate instruction on new equipment. This is time wisely spent since a well-trained staff is not as likely to misuse equipment and cause unnecessary repair costs. Since it is the secretary who best understands the overall operation of the office production unit, is most familiar with existing problems, and can best discern solutions, the secretary is also best qualified to be involved in planning the office work space.

One of the most important factors to be considered in office design planning is rental cost. With the phenomenal price per square foot of office rents, efficient utilization of space is a top priority. This cost element should be kept firmly in mind when making changes in the office, whether changes are the result of a move, a major renovation, or the purchase and arrival of new equipment and furniture. Rewiring and relocating furniture may be necessary for computer networks, for newer computer-based telephone systems or for transferring filing systems from manual to electronic.

Is Your Work Space Sufficient?

Take an objective look at the existing office arrangement BEFORE office renovation, moves, and automation changes take place.

Do you find yourself doing a lot of unnecessary leg work, moving papers from one end of the office to the other and back again? Do you really use that extra chair, table or file cabinet? Is the copier located conveniently for those who use it most? Is the telephone within easy reach of the person responsible for answering it? Would a better arrangement of furniture and machines streamline the flow of work, increase overall productivity, and cut costs? If your answer is yes to any of these questions, chances are the office layout can and should be improved.

Hiring a professional space planner is an option, but fees can be substantial for such services. In many cases, furniture and equipment vendors will make suggestions for your office without charge. However, if you decide to supervise your own rearrangement, here are a few guidelines:

- Make a sketch of your office space on graph paper. Scale present furniture (desks, files, equipment) and cut rectangles to scale for each piece. Position them on the graph paper to show your present layout.

- With pencil (you want to be able to erase), draw lines tracing some of your daily activities. For example: To transcribe a letter, you may frequently leave your desk, walk to a file across the room, return to your keyboard to finish the letter, go to the copier, return to your desk for picking up an enclosure before inserting and finally go back to the files to file a copy of the letter. Get the idea?
- Continue drawing lines for other daily activities. If you get a lot of criss-crossing lines, you need a more efficient office arrangement.
- Move your rectangles and draw lines following your activities as outlined above. Continue until you eliminate most of the original pencil lines.
- If you have graphics capability on your computer, experiment with different layouts. It makes an interesting game.

After planning the new layout, consider these aspects.

- Plan well in advance for rewiring telephones. You may discover that several weeks are needed just to move a phone across the room. If major new phone equipment is being installed, a longer advance time is required.
- If your company makes lots of long distance calls, investigate the long distance rates offered by various companies in the market.
- When moving phones to new locations, avoid as much unnecessary movement of people as possible.
- Installing adequate utility outlets for new equipment also requires advanced planning. Your local utility companies can help you in placing new outlets for maximum efficiency. Also, discuss with them the possible need for surge suppressors, a mechanism that protects automated equipment from fluctuations in electric voltages.

- Moving also provides an opportunity to separate certain co-workers who have a tendency to socialize too much. Relocate their desks on opposite sides of the office.

Take into consideration the ideas of everybody in the office. Ask your boss and other staff members for their suggestions since the office layout affects the entire team. By discussing furniture placement before a move, one secretary I know discovered that a staff member had feelings of claustrophobia when working in an office without windows; another employee had allergies that were aggravated by being near air-conditioning vents. By placing the first employee's desk in a larger office where the outside was visible, the claustrophobic employee left his desk much less often. The allergic staffer's desk was placed away from heat/air vents in the new office, and consequently, she missed work less. In both cases, discussion of the office move resulted in increased productivity.

By asking every member of the staff for their daily activity pattern, you will build morale and boost office efficiency as well as use work space more effectively.

The Economics of Ergonomics

Much is being said today in the office equipment industry about ergonomics, certainly not a familiar word a few years ago. Ergonomics, the design or engineering applied to automated equipment with the operator in mind, is nevertheless gaining in popularity in our man/machine environment. No one can sit in an uncomfortable position for an extended time and give his best performance. Since the ease of use and the comfort of the office equipment operator relates directly to efficiency and productivity, ergonomics is really a matter of economy.

Getting equipment to do exactly the jobs demanded of it cannot be isolated from other elements, such as the space allotted the equipment, the equipment design, and the way it fits into the traffic flow that is already established for the rest of the office layout. Keep these points in mind as you plan for new or enhanced lighting, decide the location of a copier or computer printer, or purchase of new furniture or filing systems.

Office lighting plays an important role in worker fatigue and eyestrain. Poor lighting will definitely reduce overall productivity, which in turn affects the company's economy. When selecting equipment, look for features like glare hoods and movable screens. When moving your scaled models around on that piece of graph paper, be aware of glare and reflection in relation to desk location. Also remember that light patterns change during the course of the day.

Noise is a problem everywhere these days, and the typical office is no exception. Modern typewriters no longer clatter away, but copy machines and printers do. Office personnel forced to work close to either of these noisemakers report that concentration suffers and headaches abound. If you plan to move to a larger location, perhaps a separate room can house these machines. If you are severely restricted in your present quarters, sound barriers of another sort (partial partitions, carpeting) can greatly reduce noise levels.

Recently I visited an office and noticed the operator of the word processor with arms so awkwardly extended to reach the key pad that I thought I was in a Jazzercize class. With the variety of office furniture available today, no secretary should be uncomfortable. A good secretarial chair should be adjustable, both in height and in the support it gives to the user's back. There are even chairs available that encourage correct posture, and adjustable, movable computer units for handicapped persons are now being sold. Desk tops are available that adjust for height and angle. Movable keyboards are an excellent feature since they allow the operator greater flexibility when using a terminal.

Ergonomics is important to the comfort, well-being, and productivity of the worker in the modern office. In a sense, ergonomic is as economic as the proper use of the office space.

Place Video Terminals in the Right Light for Sight

Much attention has been focused on visual problems stemming from constant use of video display terminals (VDTs). Increased computer usage has, of course, brought about a proliferation of VDTs and an accompanying increase in complaints of headaches, blurred vision, and tired eyes. Here are recommendations for selection and placement of word processors and computer terminals in the office:

- Purchase video display units that can be tilted to eliminate glare.
- Place VDTs under recessed lighting when possible.
- Windows should be outfitted with drapes and blinds.
- Choose dull finishes for walls and office equipment.
- Select desk lighting that is no more than three times brighter than overall room lighting.
- To facilitate eye focusing, arrange work areas so that VDT operators can look up and across the room.

Get the Most Mileage Out of Your Copier

Even though there might be a technical reason why the secretary cannot choose the location for the office copier, who knows more than the secretary that careless operation of a copier can result in skyrocketing paper bills, not to mention the havoc that occurs when users discover an ''out of order'' sign on the machine. Most secretaries guard their copiers from inexperienced users as they would other valuables in their office domain.

Pass along these cost-cutting and timesaving techniques to others on your staff so that you get more mileage out of the copier without abusing it.

- Always check the number of copies the machine is set to reproduce before you begin copying. Failure to do this is a major cause of paper waste.
- Learn how your copier reacts to light originals, colored backgrounds, etc. In most cases, your vendor will offer a training program. This cuts down on expensive experiments.
- Instruct every user on correct operating procedures. Mount large posters on the wall in back of the copier that offer basic instructions. Users will not have to consult the operating manuals all the time.

- Check the toner, developer, paper, etc. each morning so that interruptions do not occur later in the day.
- Dirty equipment means dirty copies and more wasted paper. Do not overlook frequent cleaning by your service contractor.
- With certain plain paper copiers, ''fanning'' the paper and inserting it with the curve up will avoid jamming the machine. This is an old technique used for earlier copiers, but it still works with many newer machines.

As you work with your copier, you will discover tricks to produce neater copies, save paper, and increase office efficiency. Add these to your list.

- If you decide to tear off the bottom of a document you do not want to copy, DO NOT FOLD before copying. On most copiers, folding causes a line to appear on the copy. Instead, make a ragged tear across the paper. No line should appear.
- To block out a line or a word, etc. on the original before copying, cover it with a ragged-edged piece of blank paper strip. Glue or tape the strip to the original to avoid slipping during the copying process. Again, the ragged edge should eliminate a line appearing on the copy.
- For multiple copies of an original that is only a half sheet, make a copy, tape the original to the bottom and copy two on a sheet. Use a cutter to separate them neatly and evenly.
- Be creative with your copier. Copy a logo or related picture that will complement your memo; cut it out and tape it to the original for multiple copies. You might even find just the right sketch from ''clip art''—packages of sketches that may be purchased and used free of copyright laws. That personal touch will make your document more attractive and eye catching. A picture is often worth a thousand words.

In spite of the other automated marvels, the office copier holds its own as ''King of the Court.'' You will get a lot more mileage out of it if you keep it working as part of your corporate kingdom.

Another Time - A Different File

Who had the nerve to say the office is paperless! As if office copiers were not enough, computers and word processors make it possible to create new documents at the rate of one million per minute. What is frightening is that someone has to do something with this mountain of paper, and this someone is usually you! It is hard enough to keep files to a reasonable size without the added bulk of catalogs, users' manuals, annual reports and computer printouts. Shoving them into the back of that gray file cabinet will not work; it is already FULL! Considering the exorbitant cost of office space and the inefficiency of older files, who needs another file cabinet?

In today's information-based society, everyone in the office is involved in some form of records management. The person who most welcomes a system that takes the drudgery out of filing is the secretary. I used to loathe that boring and unchallenging part of being a secretary. ''Miss File'' has undergone a ''facelift.'' Now, mechanized filing systems use storage media such as tapes, disks, cards, microfilms, and microfiche that provide speedy storage of information and quick access to and retrieval of data.

Another advantage of the new electronic systems is that they provide file security without taking up valuable floor space. Since Congress passed the Freedom of Information Act and the Privacy Act in 1974, file security has become vitally important. Not only must records be secure and protected but careful screening should be made of individuals who request access to records.

Sophisticated, electronic filing systems are not the answer for all offices, however. There are other cost-effective ways to handle traditional files. Instead of the conventional filing cabinet, staffers may opt for an accessible file that can be used from all sides by several people simultaneously. This is especially recommended for material that must be referred to several times each day. Invoices, bills of lading, and other active customer records that need to be quickly accessible—often the backbone of customer service—fall into this category.

Color-coded filing systems can cut sorting and retrieval time as much as fifty percent over straight alphabetical systems. These systems are economical and efficient for small, expanding or large filing systems. Letters and numbers are assigned to colored labels or tabs, and these tabs are affixed in a particular position to the file folders. The labels or tabs on folders already filed in drawers or on shelves create a color pattern which shows instantly where to file the folder. Misfiles are quickly apparent.

End-tab folders and guides are used for open-shelf filing where records are stored in horizontal rows rather than in file drawers. This system is preferred where entire folders are pulled, daily look-ups are less frequent, and records are retained for long periods. End tabs (or side tabs) are affixed to, or are a part of, the short edge of the folder or guide body. Thus, tabs are easier to see at various shelf levels. End tabs come in many types, cuts, and positions and can also be color coded.

Hanging or suspension folders that hang on special frames inserted in drawers provide easy access to even the heaviest files because the folders ride in their frames. The hanging feature eliminates sagging folders.

For bulky, unwieldy items, there are box-bottom folders—flattened and reinforced—to suit any need. These make it possible to have bulky items right along with your active files for frequent reference.

One law of good filing is to subdivide sections using an adequate number of signposts in each drawer or shelf. In a large correspondence file, the first drawer probably contains folders beginning with the letter "A," which do not save much time when you are looking for file "Am." However, if every few inches behind the main "A" designation, there is a section breakdown of "Ab," "Ac," etc. thumbing through becomes less a chore. Guides for subdividing other sequences—

- Months subdivide to days
- States subdivide into counties and/or major cities

- Numbers subdivide to decimals or alphabetical modifiers
- No fewer than 20 guides to a drawer
- No more than 10 file folders behind a guide

Computer printouts can be cumbersome beasts. They are often piled on window sills, stacked on top of filing cabinets and bookcases, or often crumpled and destroyed when forced into file drawers where they do not fit. Manufacturers of filing equipment have come up with several solutions. One of these is a binder-like, hanging folder with convenient handles that can be filed like any other active records file. This type handles like a briefcase. A number of portable file cabinets on the market are specifically designed for moving computer printouts around.

Whether traditional filing cabinets or shelf files are used, all offices need to consider the following items in establishing a new system or revamping an existing one:

- Always allow for expansion.
- Do not overcrowd folders. Either clean out a too-full file or start a second folder.
- Have a regular schedule for cleaning out files and designate a place for storage of inactive files. There is no reason to clutter active files with material that is better placed in the company archives—accessible but out of sight.
- In most cases, files should contain correspondence from the past six months that is used on a daily basis. Inactive files are usually between six and twelve months old and used less often.
- Remember to use a marker to indicate the location of a file that has been removed so that it can be returned to its proper place—a small but timesaving detail.

You might devise filing systems of your own to take the drudgery out of this necessary chore. Another time—a different file.

Micrographics —Another Secretarial Friend

One of the most popular innovations in storing massive amounts of valuable records over long periods of time is micrographics, definitely a secretary's friend. This technique allows storage of records in reduced size on microfilm. The reduced-size records are called microforms. Available in two basic formats, roll and flat surface, microforms are probably one of the most effective ways to save valuable space.

Single-frame lengths of microfilm mounted on special cards are called aperture cards. Microfiche, among the most common microforms, is a sheet of film on which many images are laid out in a grid pattern, with reduction ranges of up to 90 times.

The standalone rotary-type file is another basic system for manually storing and retrieving information that has been converted to microfilm. Computer-output microfilm (COM) and computer-assisted retrieval (CAR) are other systems of micrographics. Micrographics features more diversity as the technology progresses. Some benefits included are these:

- Space savings
- Rapid information retrieval
- Greater file security
- Decreased duplication and, thus, lower duplication costs

Before installing a micrographic system, consider the large initial expense. Secondly, remember that indexing must be done by a highly competent person in a uniform manner if information is to be easily retrieved.

Whatever system your office uses for records management, the more highly computerized, the better for the secretary. With the advent of image scanning technology, local area networking, and improved film encoding techniques, records management ''ain't what it used to be.''

Spring Cleaning— Once a Month for Desk Efficiency

With equipment properly placed and a file system established, consider the orderly arrangement of the desks in your office. You will not only ensure a professional office appearance but increase efficiency as well. In addition, whether you have your own personal desk or share several desks with others, secretaries are usually responsible for keeping their bosses' desks neat and tidy. Once a year is not enough for desk cleaning. Once a day is not enough if your boss generates huge amounts of paper and is engaged in five or six projects simultaneously.

Many secretaries prefer an arrangement similar to the one described below.

- Desk top—Calendar, memo pad, incoming and outgoing file, pen and pencil set. Depending on space availability, some secretaries prefer keeping reference books, such as dictionary, thesaurus, shipping and postal guides, post office directories, office procedure manuals, and users' manuals on the top of the desk for handy reference during the day. Tape your "action card" or "Menu" instructions for your word processor or computer to your desk until you become completely familiar with your system. If your desk has a clear glass or plastic top, place frequently-used items (zip codes, emergency phone numbers, etc.) under the glass. If you have a telephone on your desk, message forms are a MUST even if you have to create your own.
- Wide Center Drawer—Though not found in newer office furniture, the center drawer usually contains trays for pencils, pens, paper clips, rubber bands, scissors, tape of various kinds, and "Post-its.® "
- Top Drawer—(1) Work to be completed, (2) Work for slow periods (I know your reaction—"Are you kidding?"), (3) 3x5 card file of names and addresses of primary business contacts, (4) Telephone numbers of frequently-called clients.
- Middle Drawer—This should be used for stationery. Partitions usually make it easier to find various forms and preserve the condition of the paper. There should be slots for both large and small envelopes.
- Bottom Drawer—Reference books can be

placed here if you do not want them on the desk top. The bottom drawer is also the spot for miscellaneous items such as a purse for a female secretary or perhaps cleaning materials.

Desks have a habit of becoming dead storage space. Find shelf space in a closet or other storage area for items that you rarely use. Keep your work area uncluttered.

Many secretaries take pride in caring for their employer's desk. Do not be too quick to throw out someone else's materials, but do take the time to sort through papers and place them in logical sequence.

A local attorney confided in me that he had a real problem with laying things down exactly where he finished reading them. His law office had documents strewn from one end to the other, including his personal rest room. His comment was "I could never be ready to go to court if it weren't for my secretary who straightens up my desk and sorts my papers several times a day. She puts legal briefs, correspondence, memos, etc. in separate piles on my desk as she collects them from a chair, bookcase, sofa, etc. where they were deposited by me."

Be sure to keep your boss's desk generously supplied with sharpened pencils, rubber bands, paper clips, etc. Keep appointment books and calendars open and up to date. Remove extraneous materials from the desk top. Make a notation of uncompleted and overdue items that have been stashed away in a drawer.

Check office supplies regularly and make sure that there are adequate amounts on hand. Nothing is more irritating than to run out of typewriter-correction tape, have the printer tell you the ribbon is out, or realize that the floppy disk is full and there are no more.

Office supplies are a little like fashions, they are constantly changing. A well-informed secretary should stay abreast of new office supplies and equipment on the market. Frequent visits to the office supply store will generate ideas about newer items compatible with your current equipment.

Office Relocation Can Be Easier?

Whatever the reason for moving an office, relocation in a new building, a promotion for the boss, or the not-uncommon occurrence of the secretary moving up within the firm, the responsible secretary can make the transition smoother for all concerned. Note these suggestions:

- Carefully study the new office space with regard to square footage, furniture, and equipment placement. Compare this to the size and shape of your present quarters and make your recommendations for improving and upgrading the furniture and equipment.
- This is an excellent time to purge files and study the possibility of updating your system with lateral shelf files, microfiche, or an electronic records management system. As mentioned earlier, keep in mind the cost per square foot of office space; an inch saved is an inch earned.
- Take the time to duplicate your rotary file. Like most secretaries, you probably have a 3 x 5 file box or rotary file for listing names, addresses, and phone numbers of people your boss does business with, plus other important data. Before moving, update and duplicate this information.
- If your move involves file folders, take the same steps in transferring them that you would in moving them from active to inactive files.
  - Assemble and label transfer boxes obtained from your office supplier.
  - Prepare a list of clients who need new folders.
  - Type and label new folders.
  - Discard previously transferred records that are no longer needed. Be sure to GET AUTHORITY TO DISCARD IN WRITING.
- Order new stationery prior to the move. Be sure to consider the time needed for special orders.
- Notify contacts of the change of address well in advance—not a time-consuming chore if organized properly.

- Remind your supervisor to notify the firm's insurance company of the new location before the moving date.
- Notify the post office.
- Have post cards printed with the announcement of the change of address and the date the change is effective. Example:

> Effective on ______________________
>
> THE XYZ CORPORATION
> 1234 WASHINGTON FREEWAY
> ANY CITY USA 00123
>
> will be located at its new address
>
> 5678 LINCOLN BOULEVARD
> SAME CITY USA 00123

- Each day set aside a certain amount of time to address change-of-address cards if the number is especially large. If addresses are done on a typewriter instead of a word processor, duplicate them on self-adhesive labels for use in an address book to take to the new office.
- Also notify local businesses, the Chamber of Commerce, Better Business Bureau, and other civic and professional associations to which your boss or company belongs.
- Notify the company's credit card organizations.
- Go over current club memberships and subscriptions for publications received by your boss. If any are to be canceled, write a letter of notification. Send the rest change-of-address information.

• If the move is to larger quarters, and most moves are, now may be the time to ask for special considerations such as a small room for the coffee pot and a refrigerator or perhaps a table to accommodate the "brown baggers."

> Not only will this upgrade the atmosphere of any office by keeping food out of sight, it could even help eliminate the "martini lunch bunch."

Finally, KEEP THAT SECRETARIAL COOL. You are the one who can make the office move easier.

CHAPTER 4

The Office as a Community

A community is like a ship; everyone ought to be prepared to take the helm.
—Henrick Ibsen

Super Supervisor

Secretaries have a front row seat to the overall operation of the office as a community as well as a production unit, and this includes observing attitudes, actions, and interpersonal relationships among the entire office staff. Whether ''supervisor'' happens to be the title, most secretaries are in the position to become SUPER supervisors.

Good leadership is based on the ability to make people want to follow voluntarily. Leadership depends on the followers. If the office staff does not want to follow a supervisor's lead, the supervisor is not a good leader. The following suggestions will help you assume a strong leadership position:

- ''Try to always have a pleasant attitude and sunny personality. It rubs off on other people, and they are more liable to help you when you are in need of information, services, etc.'' This excellent advice was contributed by Patricia A. McCarthy, a training officer for the Federal Government (and a former student of mine.) For example, be especially friendly to service repairmen, i.e. offer them a cup of coffee while they repair the copier. The next time you need repairs, see if you do not receive high priority.
- Pull instead of push—you will get a better response.

- Avoid threatening, prodding, reprimanding and goading.
- Instead, show workers how to be more productive. Demonstration is the best teacher.
- Do not be afraid to compliment workers for a job well done. They will be encouraged to do more.
- Let workers know that they are an important part of a team and that their work is valuable to the operation of the entire organization. This includes part-time as well as temporary workers.
- If a worker is not doing well, do not become annoyed too quickly. Try to find out why.
- Provide strong direction and others will follow your lead—after all, you did not become a supervisor without having leadership ability.

Decisions, Decisions, Decisions

Each day presents new decisions for executive secretaries and administrative assistants. Here are five logical steps for decision-making that can work for you:

(1) Define the problem

(2) Analyze the problem

(3) Develop possible solutions to the problem

(4) Select the best solution

(5) Make the decision and act on it

Clear and rigorous thinking is required to define the precise problem. Narrow down the situation until the problem comes into focus.

Put the problem in proper perspective by gathering all the facts that have a direct bearing. Disregard facts that stray from the point and that might lead to a faulty decision.

For almost every problem, there are several possible solutions. Sometimes the most reasonable decision is to take no action at all or, at least, no immediate action.

In selecting the best solution, weigh carefully possible gains against possible losses; also consider the timing of the proposed action.

One secretary, acting as office manager, had a real

concern about the distribution of the work load. It seemed that some office staffers were always working conscientiously and industriously to finish their assigned work while others, working in a more leisurely fashion, never seemed to finish their work but they had plenty of time to socialize. Those who were doing the excellent work were, of course, the ones management called upon to do more extensive projects. The ''sociables'' successfully dodged greater work demands.

The problem in this office was clearly defined, and the executive had left the decision as to the solution of the problem up to the office manager. In solving the problem, the office manager considered the following courses of action:

- Fire those who were ''goofing off'' even though finding and training replacements could be troublesome.
- Call all staff members together, explain that the workload is not being equally shared and plead with those responsible for the problem to improve. (This may or may not improve an existing situation but at least it gets the problem out in the open—though it may create hard feelings among staff members.)
- Redefine the job descriptions and workloads for the entire office.

The office manager decided on the last option, even though it meant extra time and effort on her part. In so doing, she gave new titles, job descriptions, and job assignments to each staff member. All this was incorporated into a procedures manual and each staffer was given a copy.

The outcome was favorable in that members of the staff were flattered to have a title, and each knew exactly what was expected. The problem was defined, analyzed, and a solution was chosen and acted upon. According to this secretary/office manager, it worked. Above all, remember that these preceding steps are valueless unless they lead to ACTION.

Is Flexitime, Job Sharing, or Telecommuting for You?

Another decision many Americans may soon have to make is whether to share their job or split their working day. The time is rapidly approaching when many of you may have the option of working on a flexible schedule, sharing your job with another, or working at home by telecommuting, Many secretaries are already participating in these programs.

Doctors and lawyers who share offices with other professionals or police officers and nurses who rotate shifts with their colleagues have actually been involved in some kind of job-sharing or flexible scheduling for years.

For many secretaries, alternative or flexible time scheduling may better suit family and personal needs. Flexitime has appeared in several forms. The plan most often used is a variation in starting and quitting times such as starting an eight hour day at 6:30 a.m. and quitting at 3 p.m. or perhaps not coming in until 11 a.m. and staying until 7 p.m. The four-day work week is another popular form of flexitime. Some employers have also offered a half-day schedule, a one week on/one week off schedule, and even the option of taking the summer months off when children are not in school.

As telecommunications equipment becomes more sophisticated, less expensive, and more accessible, working on a home computer that is linked to an office computer is another viable alternative to working in an office. Let us take an objective look at some the advantages and disadvantages of job-sharing and telecommuting:

- Advantages of Job Sharing
  - Two or more heads are better than one. Also, if you goof, responsibility does not rest solely on your shoulders.
  - You have more time to relax and do some of the things you enjoy while still receiving a pay check.
  - Less job pressure.
  - If you are ill, your experienced partner can pinch-hit so that work does not pile up. Both you and the company benefit.

- Increased productivity.
- The quality of work improves if both partners remain enthusiastic and take pride in their work.
- Productivity is heightened when people have time to handle personal problems which occasionally arise. They can relax knowing that work is being done by another regular, responsible professional.

• Disadvantages of Job Sharing

- As in any partnership, you must share the praise and the raise with your partner.
- You may have to share the costs of fringe benefits, such as insurance, health and retirement.
- Sharing might reduce the incentive to do your best.
- It is possible that the quality of work will decrease if both partners are not enthusiastic and do not take pride in their job.
- A poor attitude on your partner's part could constitute a serious threat to your position.
- A lot of people may not be mentally attuned to sharing the work load fifty-fifty; this could cause problems as well as a work slow up.
- You may have to share with someone who is not congenial.
- A coordinating arrangement must be worked out, such as keeping a log or calling in when you are off. This could be cumbersome.
- Sometimes job sharers are the first to go if a reduction in the workforce becomes necessary.
- Career advancement and promotions may be withheld because you are not a traditional, full-time employee. With proper planning, this possibility can be eliminated.

- Advantages of Telecommuting
  - You have the flexibility and freedom to use time as you see fit.
  - Many qualified, trained personnel unable to work in an office situation are quite able to work in their homes.
  - In many cases you save money, time, energy, and stress by not driving to work everyday.
  - With fewer workers on the premise, offices save on rent, utilities, and other overhead expenses.
- Disadvantages of Telecommuting
  - Poor time management is more likely to occur in the home than in the office.
  - Telecommuters must be highly disciplined, setting their own deadlines and work methods.
  - Jobs which require sitting at a computer for long hours can cause physical stress.
  - Being out of the mainstream of the office can cause feelings of insecurity.
  - Because of the long-term deadlines for home workers, workloads tend to be greater.

Secretaries, should the choice arise in your office, you will have to decide whether flexitime, job sharing, or telecommuting is for you. Give these options a lot of thought.

Office Ethics—How much is Enough?

Just how important are ethics in the office? A list of character traits that bosses and secretaries in management consider the most important in hiring of employees would probably show honesty and integrity at the top of that list.

As defined by the American Heritage Dictionary, ethics is ''the rules or standards governing the conduct of the members of a profession.'' Certainly, honesty would have to be included as an ethical standard. Stealing computer information, for example, is a national problem in offices today. ''Time'' theft is also a type of stealing too often overlooked. Time theft can be just as offensive from an ethical point of view as from a production standpoint. Goofing off (especially when the boss is gone), consistently arriving late or leaving early, using company time for personal business, and taking unjustified sick leave are other ways of stealing from a company. Unfortunately, many employees do not consider this the same kind of theft as that of taking a blank diskette home or using company postage stamps for personal use. Is not pilfering time from the company the same as taking petty cash?

When an employee agrees to certain policies on accepting an assignment, failure to follow these policies shows a lack of integrity, a trait often missing in today's office environment. Absence of concern, commitment, and loyalty often cause failure not only of a particular project but an individual's career. Possession of these traits is what makes professional secretaries so valuable to the office team.

If an employee lacks personal integrity, no amount of skill and intelligence can make up for this want of ethics. When it comes to office ethics, too much is not enough.

Keeping Information Confidential

It is part of every secretary's job to guard confidential information from the eyes, ears, or hands of outsiders. Rarely is the secretary warned of the sort of curiosity that may be encountered within the office community. I know some secretaries who are so good at keeping company secrets one would think they got their training at the CIA. To help you keep information confidential, review these suggestions:

- Do not leave confidential papers on your desk even if they are in a folder or face down. Put them in a drawer or in your briefcase away from the overly curious.
- Always keep a folder handy when working with important documents. If someone comes into your office, discreetly slip the paper into the folder.
- Carefully guard information in your typewriter or on your computer screen. Never leave the room without taking the page out of the typewriter or temporarily clearing the screen. Also, do not hesitate to cover information in

your typewriter or screen when prying eyes try to read over your shoulder. If anyone becomes embarrassed, it should be the snooper, not you.

- Be alert to the danger inherent in all carbons (carbon paper, typewriter and computer printer ribbons, and carbon pull-outs). Destroy all carbons or ribbons since confidential information can be abstracted by anyone bound on discovering company information.
- Before leaving the office for lunch or for the day, put any confidential papers in locked drawers. A locked desk and file cabinet is the best deterrent to prying eyes.
- Keep your voice low when discussing hush-hush matters. Remember, voices carry, even behind closed doors. If someone drops in at an inopportune time, interrupt the conversation or end it as quickly as possible.
- If a co-worker asks you point-blank about a confidential matter, look as though the question baffles you. Then tell the person, "I really couldn't say."
- Pretend you are busy. If someone keeps asking for information you cannot give, tell him you are too busy to talk.
- Resist the urge to pacify someone by telling him "just a little." That "little" may be all that particular person needs to put the pieces of the puzzle together or to start a rumor.
- Take a firm stand. Do not be browbeaten; say sternly, "I'm not free to discuss that." Better yet, say, "If you really want to know, ask the boss."

The Secretary Can Help Keep Computer Secrets

With the advent of computers, employees have more ways than ever to take secret information from company files. Records security was safer when it was entrusted to the mind of the secretary than it has been in recent years, now that large files of data are concentrated in a single, minute silicon chip. Office crimes—stealing, sabotage, bribery, extortion and fraud— are facilitated by the presence of the computer. In some instances, underground networks exist that pass information to other company departments or to competitors. Fraud involving corporate information stored on a small diskette and smuggled in a briefcase, handbag or top coat pocket, is skyrocketing. To date, there is little protection against it.

In many cases, management is at the mercy of employees or outside computer experts who update and computerize offices. There are, however, measures that secretaries can take to help thwart the problem.

- Seek cooperation in establishing ethical practices concerning confidential information, and discuss the lack of integrity on the part of those who do not follow these policies.
- Identify all diskettes with date, label, code, etc. Never allow a blank diskette to float around the office.
- Keep a close check on the number of diskettes purchased and their location. An end-of-the-day check-in of all diskettes might take a little extra time but can also help eliminate theft or misuse.
- Lock all diskettes in a safe place. Most office suppliers stock various-sized diskette cases that feature a lock and key. Also consider fireproof storage. They are safer and preserve and protect your disks from more than theft.
- Establish a procedure for disposing of diskettes. Do not just throw faulty disks in the wastepaper basket. You might be amazed by what a computer hacker can do to retrieve data you thought was lost forever on a damaged disk.
- Keep a watchful eye on all data disks in your domain. Having an established system for disk security might eliminate the temptation to tamper with them on the part of some.

The Coffee Break—Food for Thought

Are there times when you feel as if you were running a catering service instead of an office? One of the biggest complaints I hear from supervisors and secretaries is their concern about the amount of time wasted to coordinate coffee breaks, run out for lunches when meetings extend into regular meal hours, and plan and stage company social events. These are, of course, part of the interpersonal relationships that are so important to the office community, but they must be properly regulated to avoid major problems affecting productivity.

The coffee break not only exists but has become a national pastime. It is also being seriously abused to the extent that phones are left unattended or manned by inexperienced operators, forcing callers to be inconvenienced. Printers run out of ribbon in the middle of a mail merge and sit dormant until the coffee hour ends. Important mail fails to go out on time. Not only is the ''caffeine caper'' plaguing the office of today, but with microwave ovens and refrigerators appearing in more and more offices, the problem could mushroom into an even greater loss of valuable time away from the work station.

As if the coffee break does not take enough time, think of the round-trip to and from the local deli after the half hour discussion of who wanted lunch with or without fries. Pity poor Secretary Sally with the coffee spills on that new silk blouse from overfilled deli cups, or Secretary Sam who is stuck with cleanup long after the meeting adjourns.

Frankly, you will have to put your foot down about office social shenanigans. Recognize that they are here to stay and must be organized like other office procedures or they will play havoc with productivity. Even though you may step on a few toes at first (even your boss's), the staff needs to be aware that you are running an office and not a restaurant; that you are getting secretarial wages and not tips, and that it is really in the boss's best interest to let you run the office as a business rather than an eight-hour social gathering.

We would all be better off (and probably thinner) if we could save the coffee, tea, and donuts for AFTER five.

When the Holiday Syndrome Hits the Office

The holiday season—that time of year when secretaries are usually called on by executives to plan a social function for the office—can be a lot of fun or a first-class headache that takes valuable time away from office duties that should not be neglected.

If you find yourself in this predicament, get specific input from your boss and other staff members about the exact type of event you are responsible for planning. It may be a simple affair held for an hour or two after the office closes or an elaborate party away from the office. Whatever the style, GET ORGANIZED. Next, GET HELP FROM OTHERS. In this way it will be a team effort, and you will not leave yourself open to later criticism. If this is the first time you have planned a social event for your office community, here are some guidelines:

- Determine what kind of event you want—a party after work, a banquet, a dance, etc.
- Decide on the time and place.
- For a large, more formal affair, you might decide to hire a caterer. This will eliminate much of the preparation, time, and worry on your part; but it will be expensive.
- Determine your budget. Is the firm picking up the tab or is the staff paying for the party?
- Once these decisions are made, DELEGATE as much as possible.
- If you decide on a simple in-office affair, consider having each staff member donate food or party items, or collect an equal amount of money from everybody and have a committee do the buying.
- You coordinate only. Let your committee do the rest.
- When party time arrives, do not let it become a gripe session, which might cause hurt feelings and embarrassment later.
- Even though spirits are high during this gala season, you have to face your co-workers the next day, so be careful of what you do and say.

Plan carefully and the affair will be a smashing success. Graciously accept the praise and thanks that come your way, and then be the first to suggest that someone else plan and coordinate next year's event.

Does the Hat Get Passed Too Often?

Once the holiday social is planned, the problem of "the hat getting passed too often" arises. Will you give the boss or others a gift? If so, what and how much should it cost? These are questions asked during the holidays and also at other times of the year. There are some simple answers to such questions.

You must consider that some members might choose not to participate. Part-time or new employees should not be pressured into contributing.

If your office has no standard policy on giving gifts, now is a good time to form a committee to set up guidelines that can be included in a procedures manual. They may include collecting (periodically) a specified amount from each employee or establishing a gift fund. You may choose to designate an amount to be spent on particular gifts—wedding, shower, retirement, Bar Mitzvah or a gift for the boss. Taken a step further, a standard gift, such as a baby album for baby showers, may be chosen for each category of gift. In this way, several gifts may be purchased at one time, especially if they are on sale, and can be held until needed.

Another suggestion is to circulate an envelope with a note attached explaining what the contribution is for and asking for donations (no set amount). An employee can elect to contribute or not. The amount given by each donor (or lack of same) remains unknown.

If it is not convenient to contribute to office collections, do not hesitate to say, "No thank you; I cannot contribute at this time." No further explanation is necessary, and no one should be embarrassed by a graceful "No."

CHAPTER 5

The Office as a Production Unit

The great thing with work is to be on top of it, not constantly chasing after it.
—Dorothy Thompson

Productivity... A Buzz Word That Will Last

Productivity is a key concern of management in business, industry, and government. Since the 1960's, as office costs have spiraled up, productivity has remained low; in fact, office productivity only increased four percent in the past two decades. Concern arises not only out of the Japanese challenge, which is formidable, but out of a lack of commitment, awareness, and maximum output on the part of employees at all levels. PRODUCTIVITY might be a buzz word, but as technology plays a larger role in the modern office, office support personnel must take on more responsibility with increased efficiency. Competent secretaries, regardless of whether they are performing administrative, correspondence, or other duties, need to set priorities, make decisions, adapt readily to the new technologies, and establish a high level of commitment as they proceed with the various tasks that keep the office productive.

Procedures Manuals Save Time and Increase Production

A procedures manual, a step-by-step how-to guide, serves as a convenient reference to answer employee questions—especially appreciated by those new with the company. Even though the company may have a general procedures manual, each department should design its own manual to suit its specialized needs.

Many types of manuals are used in offices today. User manuals for recently purchased equpiment are invaluable. These should always be kept close to corresponding equipment. One of the greatest advantages of user guides and procedures manuals is that you can take them home and study there. Be sure to return them if they are not your personal copies.

An effective procedures manual should be easy to use. Lengthy, complicated explanations take too much time to read and are often difficult to comprehend. If you are compiling a procedures manual for your office, consider the following items for inclusion:

- Procedures for Handling the Office as a Community
  - Telephone—Placing, receiving, screening, and transferring calls; how to handle long distance and teleconference calls.
  - Mail—Incoming and outgoing; postal services used, i.e. permits, meters, bulk rates, Mailgrams, etc..
  - Meetings—Arrangements, agenda, follow-up.
  - Travel Arrangements—Itineraries, transportation, hotels.
- Procedures for Managing the Office
  - Planning and organizing work schedules.
  - Supervision and evaluation of co-workers.
  - Grievance procedures.
  - Followup procedures/reports.
  - Operation of office equipment, i.e. copier, transcription equipment, calculators, and other document originators (facsimile machine, computer and computer/printer.)
  - Method of logging and measuring work.
- Procedures for Communicating
  - Formats for all administrative documents.
  - Examples of document styles in standard use, such as letters, memos, forms.
  - Proofreader's symbols/techniques used.
  - Method of coding and recording documents.
  - Use of routing slips.

In addition to specific procedures, an additional section in the manual can include the company organizational chart, company policies, employee benefits, and other information pertinent to your company's needs.

Logging Work Increases Productivity

Along with the proper design and maintenance of procedures manuals, many companies maintain an accurate record of work produced in the office. This is often supervised by the secretary and can be especially helpful for measuring productivity in a word processing center. A record of work produced can then be used to (1) evaluate the production rate of each employee, (2) develop and update standards of performance, (3) determine when additional staff and equipment are required, and (4) establish a charge-back system if your company charges various departments based on the time or units required to do a job.

The majority of log systems include most, if not all, of the items listed below:

- Disk, cassette or other media used marked with identification number.
- Date and time work is received; time of completion.
- Date work is requested, any special priorities and/or notations.
- Document originator-person and/or department.
- Kind of document: report, legal form, resolution, letter, memo, chart, graph, etc.
- Requisition number.
- Length of the completed document: number of lines, pages, or units.
- Name or initials of the secretary handling the work.
- Other items applicable to a particular office.

The Secretary's Role in Planning and Attending Meetings

As a normal function of doing business, many companies schedule meetings, conferences, and large conventions to be held out of town. The chairman or director may ask the secretary to assist in routine planning and to take minutes or less formal notes of the proceedings. The atmosphere and productivity of a meeting is a factor of efficient planning, execution, and follow-up, all of which are often the bailiwick of the secretary.

Meeting Types

To better handle responsibilities, the secretary should know the exact kind of meeting being planned. Meetings are usually set up according to purpose and number of attendees.

- **Work conference** - For planning, gathering facts, and solving organizational and program problems. These are usually small, face-to-face groups with high individual participation.
- **Task force** - A large or small group of people assigned to accomplish a specific job.
- **Seminar** - Usually a discussion with a specific leader providing expert information to the entire group.
- **Workshop** - For gaining new knowledge, skills or insights. Often an expert conducts.
- **Clinic** - For training in one specific subject area. Usually staffers from within the organization provide most of the training. Outside experts may also be used.
- **General Session** - Includes the total group before dividing into smaller groups. Any of the above may be included in a general session.
- **Work Session** - Several groups split off from the total membership to work on specific problems. A report back to the general session is usually expected.
- **Conventions** - Large scale meetings often held in large cities in hotels or convention centers equipped for such groups. Any of the above-mentioned meetings may be scheduled during a convention.
- **Teleconference Meeting** - The newest kind of meeting resembling face-to-face conferences but transmitted by communication satellites. Participants view each other on a television screen in their home offices.

Preparation Can Make the Difference

Preplanning procedures for any kind of meeting make a big difference in the successful outcome of the meeting. Proper planning creates a positive mind set and lends a professional and businesslike tone to the meeting. For successful meetings, try the following:

- Before the meeting—
  - Determine the type of meeting: stockholders, director's, special committees, task force, etc.
  - Send notices to participants.
  - Include date, time, place, and purpose of the meeting.
  - Invite participants by phone if you do not send mailed notices.
  - Keep an accurate record of all replies. If invitations are mailed, a follow-up phone call is in order if you do not receive a prompt reply.
  - Reserve the conference room if the executive's office is not going to be used. Make sure the conference room chosen is large enough to accommodate all the attendees. Check the adequacy of seating, lighting, ventilation, and electrical outlets.
  - Prepare the agenda. This is an itemized account of all matters to be included in the meeting. A typical checklist follows:
    - ✓ Read the minutes from the previous meeting.
    - ✓ Call for reports from particular officers.
    - ✓ Enumerate business of meeting. (Be sure to have supporting papers, reports, etc. with all information necessary to supply groundwork for discussion.)
  - Arrive early enough to check room and last-minute details. Arrange the physical layout of the meeting. You may provide name cards, pen and pencils, note pads, ash trays and matches, copies of the agenda, and other miscellaneous items according to

standard policy for your company's meetings.

- Provide other necessary or requested accessories, such as audio-visual aids, chalkboard, easels, microphones, etc.
- Have company by-laws, minutes of the previous meeting and all other materials pertaining to this meeting readily available.

Making Meetings Worthwhile

Unfortunately, a common reaction to many meetings is that they are a boring waste of time. A secretary usually cannot do much about this situation, but you can take measures to ensure the meetings you are involved in are interesting and worthwhile as well as productive. By following the practices listed here, you can alleviate the tedium of meetings and encourage others to follow your lead.

- By passing out an agenda, you build enthusiasm before the meeting begins.
- Be sure that ideas solicited from meeting participants are acknowledged and that some attempt is made to carry them out. People show a more lively interest when their own ideas are under discussion.
- Keep trivia out of meetings. Items that do not concern the majority of attendees should be handled separately, not in a general meeting.
- Agenda objectives should be well defined. Try to achieve all the objectives set for that particular meeting.
- Keep the meeting brief. If several speakers plan presentations, give each a time limit well in advance and stick to it.
- Stick to the subject. Do not go on to another item until you have clearly finished with the first.
- Assign certain individuals to address specific problems, formulate solutions, and report back at a later meeting.
- Do not let anyone monopolize the meeting. If this happens, immediately take over and go on to the next item.

- Before closing the meeting, give a brief summary in case anyone missed an important point.

Word Processing The Minutes of a Meeting

At some time, most secretaries are asked to serve as recording secretary at a meeting—if not professionally, then as a member of a social, church, or civic organization. It is not uncommon for the professional secretary to be asked to attend special company board meetings and take minutes for the boss. For one taking minutes on a regular basis, use of a word processor facilitates the process.

Establish a format that you like—one that suits the business of your organization and after the first minutes are stored on disk, only minor adding, deleting, and updating are necessary for future use. Here are a few guidelines about items that minutes include and how to format them for ease of reading.

- Minutes should include:
  - The date, time, and location of meeting.
  - Names of all members attending, including guests.
  - A statement that ''The meeting was called to order by----.''
  - A statement that ''The minutes of the last (date of meeting) meeting were presented and approved.''
  - Treasurer's report and any discussion that occurs concerning disposition of funds, etc.
  - Motions and the names of members making and seconding such motions.
  - Miscellaneous agenda items need not be recorded word for word, but generalized as briefly and as concisely as possible unless someone has specifically requested that remarks be recorded verbatim.
  - Resolutions must be recorded word for word. In so doing, if at any time you are unsure of what was said, that is the time to signal the speaker to repeat his remarks. At the end of the meeting may be too late.

When typing a resolution:

a) Double space the document.
b) Indent paragraphs ten spaces instead of the usual five.
c) Type WHEREAS and RESOLVED in all capital letters.
d) Margins should be 1 1/2 or 2 inches wide since the document may be matted and framed.
e) If a person is named in the resolution, highlight the name in all caps and bold type. If using the typewriter, use carbon ribbon and type over the name five or six times; a word processor can boldface type for you.

- Formatting the Minutes
  - Use 1 inch side margins
  - Begin the heading lines 1 inch from the top of the paper and center each line. For example:

MINUTES OF MEETING
Planning Board
Department of Development and Assessments

(or)

EXECUTIVE BOARD
Minutes of the Meeting
Your Town's Business and Professional Assn.

  - Single space the minutes with a double or triple space before side headings. The use of side headings will make identification of topics easier.
  - Use boldface type for side headings and to highlight dates, names, or other important items—simple to do when putting your minutes on the word processor.

- Topics for side headings include:

Membership	Old Business
Committee Reports	New Business
Public Relations	Special events
Treasurer's Report	Awards
Next Board Meeting	

- The closing "Respectfully submitted," may be used but is unnecessary. If not used, space several spaces after the last line of the minutes and type "your name, Recording Secretary" beginning at the center of the paper. Sign above your name.
- Label the diskette and keep it handy.
- Be sure to file a hard copy of each meeting's minutes if you make changes to the previous minutes instead of opening a new document.

The minutes of the meeting are like other office documents. Their preparation can be made easier by using a word processor.

Follow-up—the Real Difference

Immediately after a meeting, go over your notes even if you do not plan to transcribe them right away. Do this while everything is fresh in your mind; otherwise, the passing of time may distort what actually transpired.

When you transcribe the notes for final approval, be sure to include all the essentials that minutes of a meeting should include.

Send a follow-up memo, including meeting events and minutes, to all participants. This is helpful for those who were unable to attend, and this final touch marks the professional.

The Secretary's Role in Planning a Convention

The secretary can provide invaluable help to the boss who has been selected to plan a large scale meeting or convention. Planning—the where, the how, and the who—usually begins a year or more in advance and progresses to the convention site for the details that must be handled on location before the opening speeches are heard. Though the major decisions are usually made by the convention chairman, his secretary will be deeply involved in all stages of the planning and will find the art of delegating details a useful skill. Consider the following:

- Location—Convention Center or Hotel
  - Distances from airports and railroad stations, public transportation carriers, hotel facilities as well as recreational opportunities for participants are major factors in site selection. Other important factors include availability of office space, hospitality suites, meeting rooms and parking. Major convention cities book facility reservations years in advance; therefore, much will depend on timing.
  - Learn the names of the people who will be responsible for your meeting at the hotel and/or convention center.
  - All reservation confirmations should be sent directly to participants. Computerized systems in use today are far more efficient for express check-in and check-out, and there is less chance for error. A computerized system will relieve someone in your company (probably you) from the task of keeping up with attendees' housing.
  - Obtain the exact name or number of each meeting room; be sure the room is sufficient for the function for which it will be used. Room assignments are difficult to change once they are made.
- Handling Printed Materials
  - Once the exact date and place is established, contract for any printed materials such as signs, ballots, agenda, and programs. Have these delivered to the convention site. In case an error is made or changes are needed, there will be ample time for the necessary corrections.
  - Make sure a copy machine will be available for both staff and convention attendees.
- Meeting Rooms and Office Space Assignments

- Inspect meeting rooms well in advance to make certain they will accommodate the anticipated number of attendees.
- Check accessibility of meeting rooms to each other.
- Make sure rooms are arranged for the type of sessions to be held—comfortable chairs for long sessions and tables for writing sessions.
- Make sure that the view from the podium is unobstructed and that there are no distracting noises, i.e. too close to the kitchen.
- Ventilation, acoustics and lighting should be adequate.
- Audio visual equipment (microphones, lecterns, amplifiers) should be available and in good working condition.
- A temporary office for you to use as a control center is a must. Request an office from the hotel or convention center—make sure it is equipped with necessary office supplies.

• Registration Procedures. Quick registration procedures, with no long waiting lines, will get your meeting off to a good start.

- Arrange for adequate space in the hotel or convention center for attendee registration. Much of the secretarial detail focuses on the registration desk, which should be manned at all times.
- Provide signs for directing attendees to various locations.
- Each attendee should have his own envelope waiting for him at the registration desk, arranged alphabetically, for rapid distribution at the appropriate time.
- If possible, send registration materials to participants in advance.
- Take plenty of office supplies with you: pens, pencils, tape, letterhead stationery,

envelopes, Post-it® pads. An office supp store might be blocks away.

- Catering
  - Coffee breaks, luncheons, and banque should be arranged through the hotel with a catering service.
  - Special table effects and seating arrang ments should be coordinated with th maitre d'hotel.
  - Most hotels have printed menus and speci services for catering convention events. Sen for all such materials in advance.
- Hospitality
  - As a courtesy to all convention visitors, yo may wish to provide a brochure (most hote have them) in the registration pack explaining the amenities that can b expected such as parking and dinir facilities in the area, entertainmen sightseeing, and points of interest.
  - Provide a daily schedule of events to a hotels used by convention attendees as we as copies to the convention center for i bulletin boards.
  - A guest of honor, such as the keyno speaker for the convention, should hav special treatment. As a courtesy to the gues a staff member should be assigned to me him or her at the airport, take care of th guest's transportation, escort the guest special events and act as a tempora aide/assistant.
- Follow-up Procedures. Once the show meeting is over, a few loose ends must be tie Check with those on the hotel/convention sta that you have worked with, thank them fo their assistance, and make sure your com pany's obligations have been met:
  - Return borrowed or rented equipmen
  - Throw away leftover convention material

especially printed matter. This is usually less expensive than shipping these back. Chances are the materials cannot be used again since they were printed with dates and times tied into the meeting just ended.

- Verify and sign any bills your company has incurred before forwarding them to your company's accounting department. Do this before you leave the convention location; disputes can be handled more quickly on the spot.
- A final must is a summary of your experiences, especially if any unusual problems occurred—otherwise they might arise again. Include these in your company's procedures manual for that lucky person taking over the convention planning the next time. IT MIGHT BE YOU AGAIN.

Teleconferencing vs. Traditional Meetings

Recent developments in telecommunications involving computer conferencing, teleconferencing, and video/audio conferencing are changing the way business executives confer with colleagues. These innovations have also begun to curtail travel from city to city to attend seminars, workshops, conferences and conventions. Ultimately, many meetings which secretaries attend now may be eliminated as time goes by.

Video conferencing by satellite, most closely simulating the face-to-face meeting, is now being offered by public utilities companies such as AT&T. Color video conferencing held over ordinary telephone lines is also available.

Private firms offer studios to businesses wishing to use private conference rooms. Major hotel chains have jumped on the teleconferencing bandwagon and have established public video meeting rooms for guests. Colleges and universities are now taking advantage of satellite networks for educational purposes, many supported by privately endowed funds and corporate gifts. Some public telecommunications stations now offer video conferencing for use in training executives.

The major drawback of any form of telecommunication is cost. In addition to capital outlay for studio space and terminal equipment, there are the costs of satellite transmission.

Consider these advantages to businesses and secretaries:

- Much of the correspondence, time, and coordination required to get a group of individuals together for a person-to-person meeting—usually handled by the secretary—can be eliminated.
- Messages, notes, and minutes facilitated by computer networking can be produced and printed while the conference is in session, making the job of storage, retrieval and follow-up more accurate as well as more immediate.
- More people are able to attend a meeting held "in house." This cuts down on travel costs and time away from the job and makes participation possible for individuals who would otherwise not be able to attend.

Teleconferencing, a sleeping giant that is rapidly awaking, is very likely to replace some of the traditional meeting procedures that involve secretaries as they keep office production humming. Follow these teleconferencing guidelines:

- Coordinate times and agendas carefully, keeping in mind each individual participant's schedule.
- Plan such conferences during off-peak hours, if possible.
- Take time zones into consideration when placing such calls.

IRS Time—The Secretary Helps Get Ready

You may not be as involved in planning and coordinating meetings now that computer networks and satellites are taking over, but you can help your company get ready for Internal Revenue time. April is too late to start gathering documents for the tax accountant. The wise approach is to keep a list of the needed data throughout the year. Listed below are typical documents the accountant will request (especially if the Internal Revenue Service has requested an audit of corporate returns):

Articles of Incorporation	Sales Journal
Corporate Minutes Book	Disbursements Journal
Stock Certificate Book	Voucher Register
Copy of Adjusting Entries	Inventory Records
Payroll Tax Forms	Invoices covering capital items
Accountant Worksheets to tie general ledger to tax return	Copy of Prior Year's Return
Copy of Return(s) for affiliated company(ies)	Copy of Major Shareholders' Returns

According to some Certified Public Accountants, one of the most neglected of all items is the corporate minutes book. A required formality for corporations is keeping minutes of shareholders' and board of directors' meetings. The company attorney is best qualified to advise on items that should be recorded and the proper wording of those items. The following are generally included in the minutes book:

- Officers' salaries and bonuses
- Bonuses for other employees
- Annual shareholders' meeting and the election of directors
- Welfare and pension plans, including hospitalization, group insurance, etc.
- Declaration of dividends
- Reasons for accumulation of funds
- Corporate policy on reimbursement of travel and entertainment expense, especially for officers who are also shareholders
- Directors' fees
- Hiring of corporate officers
- Leases, particularly of property or equipment rented from principal shareholders
- Corporate organization or reorganization
- At least once a year, a general ratification of all acts of directors and officers

With proper planning and continuous recordkeeping, office production will not be forced to slow down while everyone frantically rushes around the office getting ready for April 15.

Planning the Business Trip

The busy executive spends an enormous amount of time traveling. While travel arrangements may be made through a travel agency, the secretary can be of inestimable value by anticipating the boss's needs for the trip and preparing the office for his absence. To make the trip easier, here are a few tips:

- Prepare a list of travel information: (1) Destination, (2) preferred travel method (plane, train, or car), (3) priorities of speed and economy, (4) date and desired time of arrival and departure, (5) type of accommodations.
- If you use a travel agency—the easiest and quickest way for making travel arrangements—give the agency complete information about the traveler: phone numbers and addresses, for both home and business. You might also want to make arrangements to pick up tickets from the travel agent.
- There are four ways to get information about air transportation:
  - Call the travel agency preferred by the company.
  - Use one of the new, on-line computer travel database services available—they allow a secretary to access (on her own computer VDT) the same information that is available to travel agents.
  - Call the airline directly and request a timetable.
  - Use the Official Airline Guide (OAG) (published four times a year by Dun and Bradstreet, 2000 Clearwater Drive, Oak Brook, Illinois 60521). The guide lists U.S. and Canadian cities and provides information about the airlines servicing those cities. Use this preliminary information to make

reservations. The OPG also indicates car rental firms and/or air taxi services.

- Some bosses prefer railway travel. Look up train schedules in the Official Guide of the Railways (published monthly by National Railway Publications Co., 424 W. 33rd Street, New York, NY 10001). Timetables of all railroads and steamship lines in the U.S. and descriptions of accommodations offered by each are listed.
- Ask your travel agency to save outdated publications—use them for phone numbers, addresses, and maps. A copy of an airport map or map of the city to be visited, clipped to the boss's ticket folder or itinerary is a real service. The North American Travel Planner and the European Travel Planner feature maps of major cities, maps of airports in major cities and car rental locations in proximity to the airports.
- If your employer prefers that you make hotel reservations, get detailed information from the latest editions of The Hotel Redbook (published by the American Hotel Association Directory Corp., 221 West 57th Street, New York, NY). It lists hotels by city and state, rates, etc.
- Be sure to take time zones into consideration when you arrange travel schedules and appointments. For hotel reservations, be sure to note check-out times and coordinate that data with other travel arrangements.
- Always ask hotels/motels for written confirmation and give it to your boss before he leaves. To be safe, re-confirm plane reservations.
- Make a checklist of materials that your employer will most likely need for the business trip.
  - Schedule of appointments. Be complete. Include name and address of company and individual to be visited, phone numbers and any special remarks.
  - A typed itinerary with dates and times of

arrival and departure, cities, method of travel, airport or railway station, hotel, alternate flights or trains that may be taken if the scheduled flight or train is missed. (The travel agency can provide this.) As an extra courtesy, prepare a copy of this itinerary for the spouse.

- Necessary information on companies to be visited. Make a folder for each company and include copies of past correspondence, letters, memos and other documents concerning the reason for the trip.
- List of credit card numbers, including telephone credit card.
- Office supplies for the briefcase, along with notebook for recording travel expenses.

Absence of the Boss

A dedicated secretary is the best insurance an offic can have when the boss is away on business, vacation or absent because of illness.

- Before the Boss Leaves the Office
  - Check all office calendars for appointments luncheons, or other activities involving th boss during the absence. Discuss with hin those events that should be reschedule after his return.
  - Notify others, inside and outside th company, who may be affected by the boss' absence. They may need to consult with hin for instructions on important matters tha might occur while he is away. This i especially true for an attorney who may hav to brief an associate to represent him in court case.
  - Check your tickler (pending action) file fo any correspondence or reports coming du during the absence. Obtain necessar instructions from the boss on what action t take.
  - Ask your boss what information to give t callers, visitors, and other staff membe during his absence.
  - If your boss is giving a presentation

making a speech, make several copies of it; give one copy to your boss and tuck the other copy inside his briefcase in case the first copy is lost or stolen. These things do happen. A secretary/administrative aide to a congressman, who makes a lot of speeches—and who has a habit of losing things—tells me that he always mails a copy of the speech to the hotel so it will be there upon the congressman's arrival. Keep a third copy in the office as a backup.

- Check with your boss to see if there are any special reports or correspondence he would like forwarded to him should his trip be extended.
- Make sure the boss signs any documents that will require his signature while he is away, i.e. checks, forms, reports.
- Keep a copy of the boss's itinerary, including his stops and phone numbers where he may be reached.
- Be sure the boss has his tickets, credit cards, itinerary, etc. before he heads out the door.

• While the Boss is Away

- Keep all the boss's mail organized on a daily basis and labeled: (1) Immediate Action, (2) To be Answered, (3) Answered by Secretary, and (4) Read for Information and Filed.
- Maintain a telephone log of all calls, including (1) Date call received, (2) Nature of the call, (3) Phone number for return call, or (4) Action taken by the secretary. Put all information on your word processor if possible for quick, easy access and for daily additions.
- Maintain a visitor's log in much the same way as the telephone log is kept.

• When the Boss Returns

- Resist the temptation to "pounce" on your boss as soon as he arrives back, and hold back others in the office from doing so as well. Let him catch his breath first.

- When he is ready, the boss will fill you in on information about the trip that you should know. In turn, bring the boss up to date on the contents of your phone and visitor logs, as well as going over his mail that you have organized.
- Update your files with new data that your boss may provide from his trip (names, addresses, and phone numbers of new business associates.) Replace any documents and papers that were taken from the office files for your boss's use during his trip.
- Process all travel vouchers, expense accounts, and receipts you are responsible for as soon as possible. Uncle Sam may need them some day.
- Inquire if your boss would like you to write thank-you notes for his signature—or he may want to write such notes by hand, especially if he was entertained at someone's private residence.

A Plan for Handling Office Mail

Among the most important of daily duties in any business is the care of the mail. Most offices have their own procedure for receiving, sorting, and distributing incoming mail, depending on the structure of the business and the volume of mail involved.

In large companies, mail is usually delivered to a mailroom where it is initially processed, delivered to departments, and subsequently to individuals. Robots are being utilized more often for this inter-company function.

Whether you are a secretary receiving your department's mail or a secretary in a small office receiving the entire load of correspondence, the following procedures will help you distribute the mai rapidly and efficiently:

- Incoming Mail.
  - Stack the mail into four piles and sor according to:

(1) Correspondence requiring immediate attention

(2) Important correspondence, not urgent

(3) Magazines and newspapers, stacked chronologically

(4) Circulars, direct mail advertising, and other trivia

- As you open the mail, write or stamp the date on all correspondence.
- Clip all enclosures to the correspondence and double check that all contents have been removed from the envelope.
- Before discarding the envelopes, make a record of insured, special delivery, registered, etc. If appropriate, staple the entire envelope to the letter for future reference. The postmark may be of significance, i.e. to the accounting or legal departments, especially if a discount is given based on remittance by a particular date. I know of embarrassing situations caused by a check having one date and a postmark another. Court cases have been won and lost over something as simple as a postmark.
- For correspondence that affects more than one person or department, make a copy and attach a note, ''for your information,'' and forward to those who need it.
- If your company's mail requires a lot of routing, start using ''routing slips'' to keep track of it.
- Sorting suggestion for your boss's mail: arrange it alphabetically unless he prefers having it sorted in order of importance or some other method.
- Use a highlighter to call your executive's attention to specific items of importance such as a particular date, deadline, or time and place of an event. The highlighted material can be stacked on top of the priority attention pile.

- Prepare a summary of the mail on a daily basis, in case your boss calls in.

- Outgoing Mail.

  Perhaps what the mail needs is not "postmen who ring twice" but senders who think twice. Whether your company is large or small, knowledge of proper mail handling, postal services available, and their utilization saves time and money and at the same time increases efficiency of handling outgoing mail. If you are responsible for most of the outgoing mail for your office, a visit with the postmaster in your area will be time well spent. Postal rates and regulations are constantly changing, and your local post office can suggest economical ways for handling various kinds of mailouts.

  - Check all correspondence before it goes out to be sure it reflects a professional-looking format, free of ink smudges or other stains.
  - Signatures should be in black ink; it reproduces better on most copiers.
  - Ensure that the letter and envelope addresses match-up. Word processor mail-merges CAN create mismatched letters and envelopes.
  - A postal scale or meter and a table of the latest postal rates are a must for every office. How embarrassing if your recipient has to pay for the privilege of receiving your correspondence.

Handling office mail is like handling all the other jobs you do so well; it requires a plan—one that works best for your office.

Handling Mail the Electronic Way

The impact and influence of electronic mail on the office environment is another adjustment to office automation that secretaries are facing. Although the U. S. Postal Service and traditional mail systems seem to be holding their own, faster and more efficient methods will soon dominate. The E-COM (Electronic Computer Originated Mail) system developed for the

U. S. Postal Service over a decade ago will soon become a reality in many offices, especially cost-conscious organizations that transmit large volumes of mail. The demand for telecommunications—the use of satellite networks—will continue to escalate in our information-based society.

Many secretaries are already involved in some type of telecommunication as they originate, produce, distribute, store, and retrieve data. The components of electronic systems consist of interface computers, word processing terminals, manager terminals, lines and modems, and, of course, software. You should be familiar with types of mail systems currently in use:

- **Facsimile,** also referred to as **FAX,** sends images other than printed and typed words, such as charts, graphs and photographs.
- **Telex/TWX,** telegraph services, varying in cost and speed, provided by Western Union Telegraph.
- **Mailgram,** an overnight service combining both the U.S. Postal Service and Western Union Telegraph services.
- **Private Telephone Processing Networks** which include (1) private, in-house systems offered in conjunction with local networks such as PBX, Datapoint, EXXON Intecomm, Telenet, etc., and (2) Computer terminals, voice and intelligence (laser) printers that are standalone in-house systems. Tymnet and Primenet are typical suppliers.
- Optical Character Recognition (OCR), the system offered by the U.S. Postal Service using scanning computers for electronic mail sorting. The latest method for addressing typewritten or computerized envelopes for this system requests the following format:
  - Use blocked format
  - Capitalize the entire address
  - Eliminate punctuation
  - Use the existing 5-digit ZIP code with hyphen followed by the four new digits.

Example: MR JOHN SMITH
AMALGAMATED NAIL AND KNOB
P O BOX 6890
MICRO CITY CA 90589-1870

(The hyphen in the ZIP is the only punctuation acceptable)

NOTE: This method was devised primarily for the benefit of high-volume mail in order to adhere to the computer and automated space limitations. The traditional method is still acceptable, especially for the individually typewritten envelope.

- In mail addressed to a foreign country, place the name of the country as the last line of the address block, two spaces below the city state and ZIP.

Example: MONSIEUR YVES DUVAL
123 RUE APIAN WAY
OTTAWA (ONTARIO) K3P0B9*

CANADA

* Coding systems vary from country to country

When the envelope contains a notation such a PERSONAL, HOLD FOR ARRIVAL, or CONFIDENTIAL, the notation should be typed in all capital letter two lines below the last line of the return address an three spaces from the left edge of the envelope.

If a notation is related to a mailing service such a SPECIAL DELIVERY, REGISTERED, or CERTIFIE MAIL, type the notation immediately under the are where the stamp or the postal meter mark is placec

If the address has an ATTENTION line, make it th second line of the address:

XYZ CORPORATION
ATTENTION MISS JANE SMITH
123 ANY STREET
KANSAS CITY MO 22260-1234

NOTE: It is suggested that the ATTENTION line b placed in the same location inside the letter instead in the traditional two lines below the letter address.

- Advantages of electronic mail:
  - Software providing more flexibility for systems to communicate with one another
  - Capability to transmit graphs and spreadsheets
  - Systems that are simpler and easier to set up than earlier, more cumbersome systems
  - Wide variety of postal services

Cost-Cutting Correspondence

Time and money-saving methods for preparing correspondence for the post office do not necessarily involve newer technology. Secretaries may want to pass these tips along to those on the staff responsible for handling the company mail.

- Use lighter weight envelopes; they require less postage.
- Eliminate retyping the address on the envelope by using window envelopes if available.
- Check the mail scale for accuracy; about one letter in eight has too much postage.
- A first-class stamp (presently 22 cents) entitles you to one full ounce (approximately three sheets of bond paper plus envelope.) Therefore, it saves money to combine mailings to the same company or individual.
- Become familiar with collection times at your mailbox. You might make the last delivery and save yourself a trip to the post office.
- Check into the remote meter resetting system which allows you to reset your postage meter by telephone linkup to a computer.
- Send a Mailgram instead of a Telegram. It is cheaper.
- Use post cards instead of letters for brief memos and letters that are not confidential. They are less expensive. Photocopy several cards at one time for your copy.
- Use the new 9-digit ZIP Code to expedite correspondence.
- Do routine letters as form letters on your word processor.

Ask your post office for other suggestions on handling special types of mail for your office. You might be surprised. Not only can you save your company money but also help to increase productivity at peak mailing times.

Part III
The Secretary Communicates

CHAPTER 6

Keeping the Lines of Communication Open

Then you should say what you mean!

—March Hare to Alice in Wonderland (Lewis Carroll)

Open Communication — Lifeblood of the Office

Nothing is more important to the smooth operation of an organization than keeping the communication lines open at all times. A prime factor leading to job promotion is a talent for written and oral communication. The secretary's professional training in communication can serve as a role model for the whole office. Here are some guidelines:

- Whether oral or written, organize instructions and present ideas clearly.
- If oral instructions involve several employees, give the message to all of them at one time so that they all hear the same words. It is difficult to repeat a verbal message the same way several times.
- Messages should be concise, complete, and correct.
- Write everything down. No human memory has enough ''bits'' and ''bytes'' to remember every detail of all events that occur in daily office operations. Use the pen; it is mightier than the sword.
- Write legibly. Poor handwriting leads to poor communication.
- Assume nothing. Just because the boss has

attended a Rotary meeting or a Fashion Symposium on the second Wednesday of each month for the past two years does not mean that he will be there for the next meeting. He might have jury duty that day. Always check.

- Avoid emotional views, jargon, slang, and buzz words. They are open to misinterpretation.
- Do not deliberately tell an untruth to anyone in or out of the office. You will lose your credibility and develop an unfavorable reputation.
- Beware of misunderstandings caused by differences in experience or backgrounds.
- Poor relationships can be turned into steppingstones instead of stumbling blocks to communication.
- The ability to listen is paramount.

The Secretary Listens

A major complaint of management is that employees do not follow directions. Following directions requires the ability to listen. Good listening, whether in a classroom, at a social function, or in the office, results in increased learning, better job and promotion opportunities, and enhanced understanding and appreciation of the spoken word.

Listening is a skill than can be acquired. Here are some listening techniques that apply to the office.

- Use your eyes as you listen. What you see when a person is speaking is sometimes as important as what you hear.
- Listen for content. Forget about delivery, especially if you are listening to an orator or are in a meeting. Professional speakers often use theatrics; do not let these tactics influence your interpretation of what is being said.
- Mentally summarize as you listen.
- Do not daydream while listening to slow speakers. Listen between the lines to tone of voice, articulation, etc. Slow delivery can be an effective delivery technique.

- Do not rely too much on memory when directions are given; take notes. Shorthand comes in handy here. However, do not get so carried away writing that you lose the content.
- Hold your comments until all directions have been given. If any part is the least unclear or questionable, ask to have the directions repeated.
- Be flexible. You might be asked to use a different approach from the last assignment. If so, follow the new instructions. Listening carefully is especially important in this case.
- Resist distractions. You might have to work hard at this in a busy, noisy office.

Regardless of the method used for communication, meaning must be transferred accurately and clearly to avoid barriers to communication.

CHAPTER 7

And the Word Was Written

Answer me in one word

—William Shakespeare

The Secretary Writes

In the beginning was the word, and to most secretaries the word was typing. It was difficult to make corrections that were neat and unnoticeable, and it was impossible to edit while typing. Now many secretaries do not type, and if they do, the word is PROCESSING, and it has become easier and even F U N ! You can move text around in a document with a simple keystroke, justify the right margin, make it straight automatically, number pages, boldface key words, center headings and columns, save text for future use, and even merge it with other information. Perhaps most important of all, you can print out your copy in original form in the most professional and pristine quality in a matter of seconds.

As word processing software evolves, it becomes ever more powerful. New software packages continue to enter the market offering programs that execute even more complicated writing and editing functions.

It is advisable to take a frequent inventory—perhaps bi-monthly—of routine correspondence and other written documents produced at your word processing center. Investigate the market to discover packages that will help you perform your job more efficiently. For example, some systems split the screen to create windows which allow you to work on several documents at one time.

Integrated packages are now available that add other functions to your word processor to prepare documents that might need graphics, spreadsheets or data-base information. It is possible to merge all this information into one system without changing diskettes.

Take a look at what available word processing packages can do for you:

- Personalize, expand, and update mailing lists.
- Address envelopes.
- Check spelling as data are keyed in.
- Point out common grammatical errors, such as misused words, overused expressions, or incorrect subject and verb agreement.
- Enhance your writing with words suggestec by a thesaurus program.
- Index, footnote, and compile a bibliography fo long manuscripts.

Programs are being improved by the removal c annoying bugs and the addition of new features. Wit a little research or a phone call (to user groups or t software manufacturers themselves) you can provid yourself with current information on all the function these programs provide and thus put a little more fu in your word processing.

The Secretary Answers Routine Correspondene

In addition to handling their own correspondenc in management roles, secretaries frequently answe routine correspondence (and some not so routine) fc busy executives. Communications include memo andums, letters concerning recommendation promotionals, inquiries, sales, and thank-you or co gratulatory messages. Whatever the nature of th business, more correspondence is being written by th experienced secretary. Some secretaries ask their boss for a list of persons who entertained them on a busine trip, and they automatically write notes expressing t boss's appreciation. Of course, they must also be ab to determine occasions that strictly require his person handwritten note. With the editing function of t word processor, letters can be written and saved a used again with only minor changes and still offer t personal touch. However, even though the wo processor performs other wonders, it cannot compose a letter with style and personality. Developing the skill of letter writing is not simple, but it can be an enjoyable and challenging task. As you write more letters, you will begin to create your own unique style or quickly pick up your boss's style if you answer his correspondence.

Here are some guides useful in making letters easier to write and read:

- First RELAX! Perhaps this is the most important technique for any kind of writing. When you start to write, phrase your thoughts as though you were going to speak. Use the simplest words you can think of—then start putting them on paper or your screen.
- Make a rough draft or outline, even at the word processor, so that you can determine whether or not you have a logical message to communicate. Try several ways of organizing ideas you want to present.
- Keep your message simple, brief, and easy to understand. Brevity, aside from being a timesaver, guarantees that the essence of a letter will not be clouded by extraneous words. Instead of saying "Due to the fact that," simply say, "Since" or "Because." "For" says just as much as "In the amount of" and is much faster to type.
- Use the YOU approach. With the "you" instead of "I" approach, you convey an attitude of respect and concern for the recipient of the letter. By all means use the person's name. There is no better way to achieve the YOU approach.
- Be POSITIVE rather than negative. It is amazing how a particular arrangement of words can accomplish this. "Please let me know if I can help you" is far more positive than "Please do not hesitate to inform me if I can be of further assistance to you."
- Choose precise words. Stay away from needless superlatives. If there is the slightest

doubt in your mind about the meaning of a word, especially with the look-alikes, consult the dictionary.

Example: She was sadly disappointed. Delete "sadly"; who was ever "happily" disappointed?

- Avoid repetition. Make your point once—clearly; it will save time and tedium for both you and the reader.
- Avoid ambiguity. Stay away from long, drawn-out sentences. These tend to confuse and lose the reader. Make sure every pronoun has an antecedent. Make sure your meaning is clear with the first reading.
- Flowery phrases are OUT. Frills and exaggerations have given way to simple, everyday language. Instead of saying "Take into consideration," say "Consider." "Assist" accomplishes just as much as "Be of assistance" and sounds less stilted.
- Keep your message conversational. If you write the way you talk, your letters will take on a more relaxed tone. The effect should be close to a person-to-person exchange.
- Do not try to be humorous. A lame attempt at cleverness can ruin the impact of your letter.
- Use a courteous, friendly tone. PLEASE and THANK YOU are simple words, but they do wonders in building good human relations on paper as well as in person.
- Make sure correspondence is complete. Many second letters are written because the first omitted pertinent facts. Be sure to check dates, numbers, times, enclosures, etc. before mailing the letter.
- Finally, check and double check for accuracy of content and technical correctness. The bottom line is to make certain the letter makes SENSE.

Handwriting in the Modern Office— YOU BET!

The moving finger writes and having writ, moves on. . .
THE RUBYIAT - *Omar Khayyam*

With the arrival of computers, word processors, and electronic calculators, you might think that handwriting is an outdated business skill. If you think handwriting is passe, you have not talked to secretaries who have to proceed through the word processing cycle consisting of revision after revision from rough drafts and changes scribbled in margins in every size, shape, and form of illegible handwriting imaginable. I hate to think of the wasted time spent tracking down the originator of a document that must be translated before it can be processed. Also think of the telephone messages taken down by hand that are unreadable.

A clear handwriting style should be required of anyone working in an office. Secretaries, wouldn't this be a great prerequisite for your bosses? What then is considered an accepted handwriting style? It is one that can be read by anyone who reads the English language and understands Arabic numerals. Any style is acceptable as long as it is readable.

If you want to test your own handwriting, write a memo to three people in your office. Give the memo to all three and ask that each read it aloud to you. If they all read without hesitation, then you receive an "A" on handwriting.

Shorthand Rusty? Brush Up

The use of shorthand dates back to the fourth century B.C. According to a FORTUNE magazine survey, 52% of middle management and 71% of top management personnel dictate some or all of their correspondence to a shorthand-writing secretary. In addition, the 1982-83 "Occupational Outlook Handbook," a U. S. Bureau of Labor Statistics publication stated, "Knowledge of shorthand is a definite plus in landing a high-paying secretarial job; many employers insist on it."

Business educators are of several minds as to whether shorthand is a dying skill. Even though shorthand may not be used in your office today, shorthand is very much alive and being used in many ways besides face-to-face dictation. The secretary who has mastered the art of shorthand dictation/transcription usually has a flair for language, a requisite for transcription as well as other forms of communication.

Shorthand is, for example, a valuable administrative tool. Telephone messages, instructions, reminders, minutes of meetings, and class notes can be recorded quickly using shorthand. Though your job may not require the skill, do not let your shorthand get rusty. Listed here are shortcuts and techniques that you may have forgotten.

- Date each day's work in longhand at the lower left corner of the page for easy reference. Red ink facilitates finding old notes quickly.
- Mark notes with a.m. and p.m. as an aid in finding notes later.
- Always use a pen to write shorthand. A pen requires less muscular effort and promotes a lighter touch. Notes written in ink are also more permanent than penciled notes. (Violet ink dries quickly and is more easily read under artificial light.)
- Use a separate notebook for each person for whom you take dictation. Place the dictator's initials at the close of each item.
- Number each item and name your document—letter, memo, report, etc.
- Cancel notes by drawing a diagonal line through each item as it is transcribed.
- Use a special mark to indicate the end of each letter. This helps you determine the approximate length of the letter when you transcribe.
- Do not attempt to erase mistakes or scratch them out. An oblique line drawn through the outline is sufficient to indicate a deletion in most shorthand methods. If this causes a problem, use a circle.
- If the person from whom you are taking dictation frequently makes changes in the dictation, use only the left-hand column of

your notebook for the actual notes, and leave the right-hand column for making corrections and special notations. This is especially helpful if you are taking the minutes of a meeting in shorthand.

- Leave several blank lines at the beginning of each new document for special instructions the dictator might mention after the dictation.
- Number each insertion in your notes, indicating its place by a caret, (^), the proofreader's symbol indicating where an insertion is to be made. A red pen or highlighter indicating insertions is also a helpful reminder.
- Keep a supply of paper clips attached to the back cover of the notebook to ''flag'' rush items, such as telegrams or priority transcriptions.
- Write proper names, addresses, trade names, and unusual or doubtful terms in longhand so that you can transcribe them accurately.
- Do not be afraid to make up your own frequent-use outlines for specialized vocabulary, names, and descriptions of company products or services.
- Use one line under words or phrases to be underscored in the transcription. (These would appear in italics in print.) Use two lines under words or phrases that are to be typed in capital letters. Three lines indicate words or phrases that are to be capitalized and underscored.
- Ask questions about the correspondence—words, spellings, figures, or other details—before you leave to transcribe it. You will avoid having to interrupt the dictator later and also cancel the risk of forgetting what you wanted to ask.
- Proofread transcribed notes for accuracy of fact and sense of content.
- Since the stenographer's notebook is the property of the employer, be sure to date and

file it in a convenient and safe place for ready reference.

- Indicate on the cover of your filled notebook the beginning and ending dates of the material it contains. Paste an index on the inside cover for double identification.

If you really wish to polish up your shorthand and also increase your dictation speed, take down the news or a speech someone is giving as you watch TV or listen to the radio. Practice, practice, practice. There is an old adage among shorthand teachers that states, ''Shorthand promotes promotability.''

Perplexed About Paragraphs?

Poor paragraphing is one of the most frequent reasons a letter fails to flow or make sense. A convenience for readers, paragraphing signals the reader that you are beginning the discussion of a new idea. The reader can follow your thinking and grasp your message. The following guidelines should help make paragraphing easier:

- A paragraph may be only one sentence, but usually a paragraph contains several sentences—all related to the same topic. Thus a paragraph may be defined as a group of sentences closely related to a specific topic.
- In the same way you limit the number of ideas in a single sentence, limit the number of sentences in a paragraph. Each paragraph should contain only sentences that deal with one topic.
- The paragraph may also be used to highlight a statement or a question. The technique of enumerating points by paragraphing creates emphasis for the reader.
- To bridge the gap between paragraphs, use connectors or transitional expressions. A good selection of linking words allows the reader to follow ideas not only from paragraph to paragraph but also from sentence to sentence. Here are common transitional expressions that help the reader follow your message:

- To Show Cause and Effect: Accordingly, As a result, Hence, Therefore, Because
- To Introduce Examples: For example, That is, Such as, Namely, For instance
- To Show Exceptions to What Has Been Said: But, Even though, On the other hand, On the contrary, Otherwise, However
- To Indicate Time, Place, or Order in Relation to What Has Gone Before: Above all, Finally, Further, Then, Meanwhile, In summary, Next, Too, Still, Also, Earlier, Later

Do not expect these aids to perform miracles, however. If your ideas do not follow a logical sequence, no transitional device will help your reader.

Which Salutations?

Salutations for the business letter may be confusing, especially if you are unsure of the sex of the person to whom you are writing. A name does not always divulge gender. What about the boy named Sue? One way to eliminate the salutation quandary is to use the Modern Simplified Letter format, (see Appendix F) which uses no salutation or closing. Current practices recommended for salutations in business correspondence follow:

• One person, sex unknown:	Dear Lynn Johnson Dear L. B. Johnson
• One person, name and sex unknown:	Dear Sir or Madam
• One woman, marital status unknown:	Dear Ms. Marr Dear Dag Marr
• Two or more men:	Dear Mr. Laurel and Mr. Hardy Dear Messrs. Laurel and Hardy
• Two or more women:	Dear Ms. Doe, Mrs. Ray and Miss Mee
• If both are married:	Dear Mrs. Doe and Mrs. Ray Dear Mesdames Doe and Ray

• If both are unmarried:	Dear Miss Doe and Miss Ray Dear Misses Doe and Ray
• If both use Ms.:	Dear Ms. Doe and Ms. Ray Dear Mss. (or Mses.) Doe and Ray (Note recommended plural for Ms.)
• A woman and a man:	Dear Ms. Mutt and Mr. Jeff
• Several persons:	Dear Ms. Ginn, Mrs. Tonique, Mr. Lime and Mr. Water Dear Friends (Romans, Grecians, Colleagues, etc.)
• An organization composed entirely of women:	Ladies (or) Mesdames
• An organization composed entirely of men:	Gentlemen
• An organization composed of women and men:	Ladies and Gentlemen

Now Which Closing for the Letter?

Closings can be as varied as salutations. The salutation phrase and the tone of the letter determine the phrasing of the closing. Here are a few closings that are traditionally appropriate, but you can be creative.

- "Respectfully yours," (with or without "very") when a letter is addressed to someone to whom great respect should be shown, such as a cleric or a public official.
- "Sincerely yours," or "Cordially yours," (with or without "very") when the salutation is "Ladies and Gentlemen," or "Dear Sir or Madam," or when the tone of the letter is formal, or distant.
- You may, of course, compose special closings,

like "See you at the convention" or "Okay, Buck?"

- Remember, only the first letter of the first word in the closing is capitalized.

How to Eliminate Sex Bias in Writing

Whether we are writing business letters, articles, or our last will and testament, many of us want to be "sex fair" but are not exactly sure about titles or proper words to use. The same situations exist when speaking, which is often even more difficult. Here are suggestions for likely substitutes:

- On form letters, use terms that apply to both sexes such as:

Dear Customer	Dear Client	Dear Policyholder
Dear Friend	Dear Student	Dear Associate

- Use titles that do not relate to sex:

  Sales Representative for Salesman
  Flight Attendant for Stewardess
  Service Representative for Serviceman
  Chair for Chairman

- When a person gives a title, use that title regardless of your preference. If the title on the letter is Ms. Patti Patriot, use Ms. even if you know she is married and you might prefer to use Mrs. Ms., as we all know, is a convenient abbreviation for either Miss or Mrs. when marital status is unknown. But Ms. can cause confusion in the plural form. I would recommend adding an **s** or an **es** just as you would to most other nouns in our language.

  Example: Dear Mss. Hill and Dale (or)
  Dear Mses. Sweet and Sauer

  If you use it, don't slight it—give it a plural.

- Female writers are encouraged to indicate the title they prefer as a courtesy to persons who will reply to a letter.

- Professional titles should be handled in the same way, regardless of sex, such as—

  Dr. Jane Doe
  Jane Doe, M.D.
  The Reverend Jane Doe

Dr. John Doe
John Doe, M.D.
The Reverend John Doe

- Some alternatives for handling situations when sex is unknown:

All female company	Ladies
All male company	Gentlemen
Female and male company	Ladies and Gentlemen

- Use position titles, such as Dear Sales Manager, Dear Reservation Clerk, Dear Branch Manager, etc., not Dear Paula Principal or Peter Rabbit.

Use an Economic Format

Now that those letters are written, if you are the one to type them, you will want to select an economical style as well as one that attractively places the letters on the page. Because office procedures, space and equipment expenses and organization of secretarial services differ among businesses, the cost to produce a 200-word letter varies dramatically. Whatever the final cost, letter production is expensive. The cost of a business letter in 1930 was approximately $.29. The average cost for a business letter today is over $8.52 and rising, according to a recent Dartnell survey. Shocked? Be sure every measure is taken to reduce the cost of producing a document. One of the first principles of cost effectiveness is, "How effective is it?" If the selected format cuts down costs by reducing operator time, it is cost effective. Here are some suggestions:

- Use standard, one-inch margins for all letters and memos. Balance the document by having your word processor move the entire document up, down or horizontally. If you are typing, pull the letter up or down by adding or deleting lines before and after the date or in the closing lines.

- Use Block Style—all lines in the document begin at the left margin. A letter with indentions, mixed punctuation, and variable placement takes longer to set up, key in and print out—even on your text editor. Although the printer is fast, extra functions add to cost over a period of time.
- Special letter parts, such as attention and subject lines, can be abbreviated, i.e. Attn: for Attention and Re: for Subject.
- Unless your company has established style requirements for salutations and closings, consider leaving them off, as in the Modern Simplified and the AMS (American Management Society) letter styles (samples in Appendix F). This also eliminates the question of which salutation and closing to use.
- For enclosures, use Enc. or Encl. instead of writing out the word. The most recent practice is to list enclosures on succeeding lines and indent three spaces from the left or begin the listing two spaces after the word or abbreviation for enclosures. Again, I would use the fastest. Here are examples of current styles:

  Encls:
     Briefing for Case 10
     Expense Report for April, 1986
     Organizational Chart

  Encls: Briefing for Case 10
     Expense Report for April, 1986
     Organizational Chart

  I prefer all on one line to save time.

  Encls.: Briefing for Case 10; Expense Report for April, 1986; Organization Chart
- Reference initials and enclosure and copy notations can be single spaced if space is needed for balance.
- If a photocopy of a letter is being sent, make the notation in any of the following ways:

Copy, or XC (for Xerox Copy), or cc (courtesy copy replacing carbon copy), or PC (PhotoCopy). Space two horizontal spaces after XC, Copy, cc, or PC before listing names.

Example: copy John Doe
XC John Doe
cc John Doe
PC John Doe

- Letters may be easily lengthened with combinations of the following:
  - Raise or lower the date
  - Leave extra or fewer spaces between the date and inside address, or between the closing and the signature line.
  - Name of sender and title may be put on same line or separate lines
  - Enclosure notations, reference initials, copy notations, and postscripts if used may be single spaced or several spaces inserted between as needed for better letter balance.
- To cut costs, use all reasonable measures to limit letters to one page. But do not overcrowd just to accomplish this.
- If the letter is longer than one page, additional pages should be on plain paper of the same quality as the letterhead used for the first page. Use the same margins as for page one.

Style 1 (3 lines for the heading beginning on line 7 or one inch from the top)

LJ CO.
Page 2
December 30, 19—

Style 2 (all on one line beginning one inch from the top)

LJ CO. 2 December 30, 19—

NOTE: Be sure to use the same date on page two as appears on page one, even if the pages were prepared on separate days.

- For interoffice memorandums, the following fast, easy format eliminates having to remember "5, 3, 3." Put the date first—anywhere after "Memorandum" or the letterhead. Use the following lines for the heading:

  RECOMMENDED STYLE: TO:
FR:
RE:

  With a one-inch left margin for the following style memo heading, the typist must indent 5 for line one and 3 before "from" and "date."

  TRADITIONAL STYLE TO:
FROM:
DATE:
SUBJECT:

  NOTE: Letter and memo format samples may be seen in Appendix F.

Processing Business Reports

Besides routine correspondence and interoffice memorandums, much business information is communicated in reports. They may take the form of legal documents, financial reports, corporate information to stockholders, or employee and company procedural manuals.

Even though report contents are the responsibility of the writer, the secretary can save time and money in completing the report by gathering and sorting information necessary to complete the document. Information required might be verification of a date, an exact title, or the complete name of an author for a supplementary part of the report. (The legal secretary is familiar with this responsibility.) It is therefore important that a secretary knows what to look for and where to look for accurate information. Reference sources include financial, professional and business directories, technical publications relating to the report, atlases, literary guides, and government publications. You may have to leave the office to gather information at the public library. To be effective, reports, like letters, memos, and all other written communication must be CLEAR, ACCURATE, and WELL ORGANIZED.

While steps in writing reports will vary from boss to boss, the secretary will no doubt be involved in each stage of the preliminary work, which may consist of a first draft and several editings or an outline listing in sequence the topics to be covered in the final report. Of one thing you may be sure, the secretary will be in on all moans, groans, yelling, and screaming if a report deadline is not met.

The majority of business reports contain three basic parts: (1) Introductory and illustrative material—title page, table of contents—tables, charts, other illustrations, and possibly a summary, (2) Body—introduction, main text, and conclusions and/or recommendations, and (3) Supplementary information—appendix, bibliography, and index.

Whether the report is brief and informal or long and complicated, the pagination-repagination and headers and footers functions of your word processor offer the easiest way to compile the final draft. Graphics software is of great assistance in preparing graphs and charts. Below are suggestions for formatting other parts of the report:

- Brief Informal Reports: These may be single or double spaced, according to the preference of the writer. The offset at the top of page one is usually 1 1/2 (nine lines) to 2 inches (twelve lines). For succeeding pages, use an offset of 1 inch (six lines); your word processor will center headings. Traditionally, side headings leave one more line space before than following them, but this, too, is a matter of space, preference and general document appearance. Side and bottom margins are usually one inch but may be wider.

- Formal Reports:Though normally bound at the side or top, some remain unbound. Margins are determined by the binding. The text is usually double spaced with five- or ten-space paragraph indentions. Side headings are the same as informal reports. Paragraph headings, if used, are indented five spaces (ten for a legal document) and are commonly underlined or boldfaced for emphasis.

- Documented Business Reports: To establish proof of material used in a report, in order to give it more "clout," writers may use source material from which data is either quoted or paraphrased. To document reports, source or discussion footnotes may be used. Source footnotes, referring to newspapers, books etc., follow the formal style. Often discussion footnotes are written in an informal sentence style. Main headings and margins for documented reports are the same as for unbound formal reports. Refer to your user's manual for instructions on how to place headers and footers; otherwise much time can be wasted staring at a blank screen or on "hold" while you wait for your word processor's service representative to tell you "how to. . ." Guidelines for keying in footnotes follow:
    - The number of the footnote should correspond to the number in the text. To indicate a footnote reference in the text, refer to "Footers" in your software user's manual.
    - Footnotes are usually numbered in sequence from the first to the last page of the report.
    - A divider line, normally 1 1/2 inches in length separates the text from the footnotes. This line may also extend from the left to right margin.
    - Double space, indent five spaces, and type the corresponding number for the superscript number one-half line space above the typing line if you are using a typewriter. Word processors usually have a superscript function. The superscript is the number appearing one line space above the text for which a footnote will be given at the bottom of the page indicating the reference source.

- Single space footnotes. If there is more than one footnote per page, double space between them.
- Footnotes are placed at the bottom of the page even though the page may be only partially filled.
- Information in the footnote includes author, title of source, edition, place of publication, name of publisher, date of publication and page number for reference.

New word processing packages are available that will automatically format a document by simply specifying the required document: memo, report, letter. This software is recommended for offices where report preparation is a large portion of the information processing.

Preparing Financial Reports

Though preparation of financial reports usually takes place in the accounting department, occasionally a financial statement must be updated and inserted into another document. The secretary working on the report will probably be responsible for this phase. Examine copies of financial documents already on file before beginning to type. Ask permission to do this if you are not directly in charge of such files. Points you should note:

- When deciding whether to single or double-space the financial statement, consider the length of the statement relative to the total document.
- Note placement of commas, vertical alignment of columns, placement of dollar signs, and single and double lines beneath figures, all of which will be automatically aligned for you by the word processor.
- Use descriptive titles to introduce groups of similar accounts. The first letter of the first word and important words in introductory titles are capitalized.
- Use of vertically aligned leaders to guide the reader's eye from the explanation column to the amounts column is recommended.

Example: July Account $789.90
September Account ... 664.00
October Account 12.09

- Consistency is an important guideline in the style of any financial report.
- Most important of all, team up with another person to carefully proofread every number of the final printout. Include the name of the person responsible for the original preparation of the financial statement in the report.

Good Proofreading Improves Productivity

The skill of proofreading is more important than ever since so much copy is proofread from video display screens or computer printouts.

All final copies must be checked in every detail for accuracy, arrangement, and freedom from spots and smudges. Your written word represents you and your company and must show the highest quality content and appearance. Consider these proofreading techniques:

- Proofread technical material at least twice. Slowly pull your document line by line down the screen on the first reading.
- When proofreading from hard copy, keep your screen and hard copy at the same place in the document. Corrections and updates on the screen will go faster.
- Read all material once for content; then read from right to left or bottom to top to spot spelling and typographical errors.
- If you are proofreading a form letter, carefully read the first letter printed out; then proofread only the variables for the remainder of the letters.
- When proofreading with dictation equipment, return to the start of the document and listen again.
- If possible, use the team method to proof statistical copy. Do the following:
  - One person reads from the original, the other from the screen. Indicate punctuation, spelling, paragraphing, format and decimal points.
  - Read numbers digit-by-digit.

- Read all columns DOWN. Read and check the numbers in the first column, then the second column and so on until all columns have been individually checked.
- Verify all extensions and totals.

Regardless of how carefully we try or how accurate our keyboarding skills, errors do manage to slip by our screen and eyes. The following are common errors (other than misspellings) to watch for:

- Words such as **if, is, it, in,** etc. are often omitted when the preceding word ends with the same letter or the next word begins with it.

  Example: (wrong copy) He serious about his work.
  (corrected) He is serious about his work.

- Be especially careful when you near the end of the screen. Many errors are missed here because the eyes are tired and strained.
- Similar words are often overlooked, such as than/then, affect/effect, not/now, or if/of.
- Confusion of suffixes sometimes cause missed errors, such as typed/types or former/formed.
- Words are often omitted at the beginning and end of lines because they are more likely to be skimmed.
- Watch for words that are ALWAYS spelled as one word: cannot, nobody, somewhat, worthwhile.
- Check the spelling of proper names, such as cities that you are unsure of, as well as two-letter state abbreviations.
- Confusion of sequence in numbers or letters is frequently missed in proofreading. Example: A, B, C, E or 11, 12, 13, 15

Errors that are caught in time by the sharp-eyed secretary speed up final production of a document, save valuable time, and eliminate paper waste.

CHAPTER 8

And the Word was Spoken

Speech belongs half to the speaker, half to the listener.

—Montaigne

The Secretary Speaks

Getting along with others as you manage the office as a community and as a production unit is the key to your success. Most ''getting along'' with others—inside and outside the company—is based on being able to communicate effectively. Secretaries constantly receive and dispense information. Making plane reservations, planning and coordinating a meeting, persuading a co-worker to accept a particular responsibility, or putting a client at ease—all require good conversational skill.

An Effective Conversationalist

To be an effective communicator, you must work at it. Becoming a good conversationalist takes longer for some than for others, but the skill can be mastered and adapted to your own style. The following are suggestions that make conversation easier with both your business and social acquaintances:

- Do not talk too fast. Slow your speaking tempo by making frequent pauses. Speaking in a relaxed manner and with clear enunciation also makes listening easier.
- Do not monopolize the conversation. Make a story short. Hit the highlights and omit minor details.
- Avoid being argumentative. Do not constantly speak out against whatever viewpoint is

expressed. A mild response is usually more effective than a contradiction.

- Keep most statements positive. Avoid unpleasant topics, criticism of others, pessimism, etc. in your conversation.
- Eliminate competitiveness in conversation. You are not trying to be a winner or loser in the conversation but a friendly part of a give and take situation.
- Maintain a tolerant and neutral attitude. A good conversationalist avoids laying down the law and preaching.
- Apply the golden rule of conversation, ''Speak to others as you would have them speak to you.''

Techniques for Speech Presentation

Many busy executives rely more and more on their experienced and knowledgeable secretaries to take over speaking duties in their absence, either in an informal setting such as the office or conference room or in the more structured setting of an auditorium. Secretaries are regularly asked to speak at training sessions for new office personnel or to give presentations to familiarize staff members with new equipment or procedures. If you find yourself in this flattering position and are unaccustomed to public speaking, do not panic. Enjoy the prestige of being asked, and begin to prepare carefully just as you would for any other assignment. You will probably receive plenty of advance notice, giving you time to prepare a good speech. The following preparatory steps may assist you if you are a novice.

Preparation

- Know your subject. If you have a choice, be sure the topic is one that you are familiar and comfortable with. If you are assigned a subject, find out all you can about it. Use trade magazines, reference manuals and other sources to assist you.
- Know your audience. Nothing is worse than to talk down to an audience. By the same

token, do not use a lot of technical terms without explaining their meaning.

- Outline your speech in an orderly sequence. Jot down each point on a 3 x 5 inch card. These may be changed around easily if you decide to rearrange the sequence of points.
- For a typed speech, use wide margins (2 to 3 inches) so your eye can move down the page without head movement; double space the speech and leave 2 double spaces between paragraphs. Many speakers prefer to type their speech on 5 X 8 inch cards for ease of handling.

NOTE: If your speech is to be printed and distributed, follow the same guidelines in preparation as for business reports and use standard 8 1/2 x 11 inch paper.

Procedure

- Choose an appropriate delivery method for your content. If you use visual aids, such as slides, charts, or handouts, prepare them in plenty of time to practice.
- Practice, practice, practice. Nothing will make your presentation more successful than feeling confident and being thoroughly familiar with your material.
- If you are using a microphone for the first time, practice with it at least once.
- If a tape recorder is available, tape your practice session and listen to it. You will be amazed at the changes you might make to improve your final presentation.
- Get a good sleep the night before. Allow time to go over your notes before giving your talk.
- Get to the presentation room ahead of time to check the setup—lights, visual aids, etc. If you are responsible for setting up, do it the day before if possible.
- Be confident. Keep assuring yourself that you have done a good job of preparing and that your presentation is going to be excellent.

- As you proceed with your speech, establish a rapport with your audience. Speak directly to them, making frequent eye contact, smiling and picking up on their responses. Adjust to their moods. It will not take long to know where you stand with your audience.
- Try not to ramble or digress from your prepared text. By getting sidetracked you risk losing the audience.
- Be prepared for emergencies. One secretary, who was to give a presentation at a Chamber of Commerce luncheon, woke up with laryngitis. She was substituting for her boss who was suddenly called out of town. Fortunately, she had duplicated most of the speech in a handout. In a whispering voice she rose and explained her dilemma, passed out the information, and gave parts of the presentation as planned. The audience was so sympathetic, attentive, and quiet that she forgot about her voice and whispered away. She received a standing ovation at the conclusion.

When your speech is over, sit back and enjoy the applause.

The Telephone—An Important Business Tool

In 1876, Alexander Graham Bell transmitted the first sentence by electric waves and set the stage for the telephone. Today, if you ask top management to rate important office skills, most would certainly rate proper handling of Mr. Bell's communication tool high on their lists. The telephone is, however, a tool that must be handled properly in transacting the company's business.

A section on the proper use of the telephone should be included in the company procedures manual. This is also a good place for a reminder that personal calls should be limited.

Telephone Personality—Create It

Even though most of us take the telephone for granted (and wish at times that the office did not have one), the professional secretary long ago discovered the importance of a pleasant telephone personality.

Listed below are telephone tactics that work for most offices. Some are recommended by the telephone company; others are suggestions for developing your own unique telephone style.

- When receiving a call, immediately do two things—answer promptly and pick up pen or pencil and be ready to write.
- Identify yourself and your company or department.

  Examples: ''Editorial Department, Miss Jones Speaking.''
  ''This is Mr. Williams office, Nancy Parker speaking.''
- Speak distinctly and pleasantly. You will find that callers like a friendly voice and will call your firm again.
- When your boss asks you to get someone on the telephone, get the person whom you are calling on the line before transferring the call to your boss. Let the person whom you are calling wait, not your boss.
- If you leave the phone to get information, explain the waiting period to the caller. Tell the caller how long he is apt to be on hold and offer to call back later with the information—then be sure to do so. Try to avoid long waits; you are holding up two business lines.
- Screen calls tactfully:
  - Find out who the caller is by asking, ''May I tell Mr. Jones who is calling, please?'' or ''May I say who is calling?''
  - If your boss has instructed you to find out each caller's business, say, ''May I tell Mr. Jones the nature of your call?''
  - Often someone else may be able to help the caller. You might want to respond with ''Mr. Jones is busy (or out of the office) at the moment, but Miss America might be able to help you.''
- If questions are phrased politely, you will more than likely elicit a polite response.
- Do not be intimidated by high-pressure tactics.

Anyone having important business with your employer will tell you what the call is about.

- Most secretaries know the names of many of the business contacts with whom the boss invariably wants to talk. In many cases you will even recognize the voice. If so, connect the caller immediately without asking the nature of the business.
- Above all, do not get carried away and become overprotective. You will learn what sounds like an emergency and put those calls through immediately.
- Know the whereabouts of your employer (and others for whom you take calls). If they are out of town, make sure you know when they are expected to return or where they can be reached.
- Take messages willingly. Be sure to get the name of the caller, telephone number, time, and whether the caller wishes to have the call returned. Repeat the information to insure accuracy before hanging up.
- By all means get the correct area code if the call is long distance; it might be someone whose number is not on file.

> Do not let this happen in your office: A large account worth thousands of dollars in profits was lost for lack of a three-digit number. The potential customer, Mr. A—, had his call answered by a new clerical staff employee who took his message. Just one problem: the new employee forgot to write down the area code. Executive B— spent untold hours and ran up a large long-distance bill trying to track down Mr. A—. Months later, at a national convention, Mr. A— approached Executive B— and informed him that he had given his account to a competitor because his call had not been returned. Executive B—, you have my sympathy.

Play it safe—repeat both the area code and phone number especially if the call is from out of town.

- Deliver all messages promptly.
- When transferring calls, signal the operator s-l-o-w-l-y. Transfer only when you know definitely that you have the correct person or extension.
- When placing a call, be certain of the number. Wrong numbers can be embarrassing and time consuming. If you are in doubt, look up the number. That is what telephone directories are for.
- Be ready to talk when the called person answers. Since most calls go through without delay, being prepared to talk is not only courteous, but timesaving.
- After you have placed the call, allow enough time for the other person to answer. It is quicker than hanging up and calling again.
- Ask if it is convenient to talk. If the person called is busy, offer to return the call at a more convenient time.
- Do not raise your voice. Shouting distorts your voice over the telephone. The instrument is tuned to normal voice levels— loud voices blur. Also, a loud voice sounds gruff and unpleasant.
- Be attentive. The person to whom you are speaking will appreciate your listening politely and attentively. You would not interrupt in a face-to-face conversation; the same rule applies in telephone conversations.
- Use your caller's name frequently. There is no sweeter music to another's ear than the sound of his own name.
- Get your thoughts in order before you call. If you have questions, list them so that you will not forget. Try to complete your business in

one call by securing the information you want or by leaving a message.

- Apologize for mistakes. When you reach a wrong number, do you hang up the receiver, or do you apologize for the mistake?
- Who should end the call? Usually the person who originates the call ends the conversation.
- Hang up gently. Slamming down the receiver is as unpleasant and discourteous as slamming a door.

Remember you are the good-will ambassador for your company. This also means while you are using the telephone. Keep those telephone voices SMILING.

The Secretary Dictates

Dictating into a microphone on a transcription machine can be as unnerving as giving a speech when you are not used to it. Clear enunciation and good speaking techniques are especially important. Traditionally, the secretary's experience with transcription equipment has been at the listening and transcribing end of the process. However, with the rapid expansion of the secretary's role, those acting as office managers can use dictating equipment to their advantage in the following ways:

- Dictate instructions.
- Cover job details and follow-up requirements.
- Dictate travel itineraries and important meeting arrangements.
- List scheduled work and assignments requiring action.
- Indicate material to be transcribed at the word processing center.

A big advantage in using dictation equipment is that it can be used when the dictator has the time—after office hours or even at home.

Using dictation equipment is an art, one that has to be practiced along with other valuable office skills. Here are some tips if you are new to the art of dictating:

- As you prepare to dictate, plan carefully what

you want to say. Organize both material and thoughts in advance. Clip pertinent data—previous correspondence, reports, etc.—to each item for dictation. Group similar items together in a "to be dictated" folder.

- Do not rush through technical material throwing in tongue twisters as you go. Remember, the person transcribing may not have the same specialized training that you have had.
- As you dictate, spell difficult and technical terms.
- Do not ramble.
- Suggest punctuation, paragraphing, and capitalization in order to make transcription accurate the first time.
- Explain changes, deletions, and insertions carefully at the time you dictate.
- Speak clearly and distinctly. Pronounce names, technical terms, and numbers carefully. These are the items that most frequently cause errors in transcription.
- As you start to dictate an item, name it—letter, memo, report. The transcriber will then be aware of the format necessary for the final draft.
- State priorities, if any, of the items you are dictating.
- When you finish, listen to your voice. If you could not honestly follow your own instructions without questions, rewind the tape and start over. It will save interruptions later when you are involved with other work.

Thus the word is spoken—and if properly spoken, THE WORD WILL BE HEARD.

Part IV
The Secretary Handles People

CHAPTER 9

The Outside World

What kind of people do they think we are?

—Winston Churchill

Secretary—The Good-will Ambassador

When you consider the number of people confronting the secretary from outside the office, you must agree that the person in this position wields plenty of clout. The secretary is usually responsible for handling office callers, screening telephone calls, dealing with the media, and often seeing sales representatives for the company. Representing your company to the outside world certainly puts you in the role of a good-will ambassador.

The Secretary Greets the Office Visitor

First impressions—whether true or false—color our opinions for a long time. That is why the secretary, as the employer's official greeter, should give every office visitor a cordial yet businesslike introduction to the company. Here are some tips on making a good impression on callers:

- The visitor who has an appointment will usually come straight to your office. However, first-time visitors, even those with an appointment, will appreciate the extra courtesy of your meeting them at the reception desk. This is especially true in large corporate offices where first-time visitors are unfamiliar with the route to your office.
- If the visitor does not hand you a business card, ask for one. It will come in handy later

for introductions and for your files. Give the card to your boss as you introduce the visitor, or put it on the boss's desk where it can be seen if his memory lapses.

- Some offices offer coffee to visitors. If it is convenient for you, offer a cup, especially if you know the waiting period will be lengthy.
- If the boss is out when a visitor with an appointment arrives, convey his apologies—tactfully but simply. Give a vague reason for the absence. "He was unexpectedly called out of the office" will do. If the visitor decides not to wait, ask if you or someone else can help. If the offer is declined, make another appointment at the visitor's convenience.

Being a gracious office host or hostess is easy when you remember that each visitor is a guest in your domain and you are the good-will ambassador.

When Appointments Run Behind: Wall-to-Wall Visitors

Some secretaries route papers; others route people. Shuttling people in and out of the office can be hard to cope with, especially if you are in an office visited by large numbers of people.

Frequently executives attend meetings and conferences outside the office and are detained in traffic. Sometimes in-office appointments run longer than anticipated. Other appointments then run behind, leaving visitors to wait in the office, often to the point of wall-to-wall people. There are several things that the secretary can do to make the waiting period a little more pleasant for the guest.

- Schedule with a purpose. Try not to set up appointments one after another; this way your boss will have blocks of time free for other duties without interruption by visitors.
- Coordinate with your boss the way visitors should be handled. You should know
  - People he will always see.
  - People he will see if his schedule permits.
  - Types of visitors he wants the secretary or another designated staff member to see.

  - A prearranged signal when callers overstay their welcome. Some bosses like their secretaries to signal by intercom when the next appointment has arrived or to walk into the office to announce the next visitor.

- Prepare the boss for appointments. To save time, be sure background data needed for each appointment is collected beforehand.
- Make every attempt to know approximately when meetings and conferences will end. Allow extra time for your boss to return to the office before arranging his next appointment.
- Send a message before the meeting or conference ends reminding your boss about the following appointment.
- Above all, remain CHEERFUL. Your good humor might rub off on an unhappy visitor.
- Forewarn people that the boss might not be able to stick to the exact appointment time. When scheduling appointments, be sure to tell the person that your boss frequently attends meetings outside the office and there may be a delay.
- If the visitor is from the area, suggest that he call you before leaving his office to see if your boss is on schedule.
- If the visitor is from out of town and has other stops to make in the vicinity of your office, suggest that he call before coming. If a problem arises, the visitor can go to another appointment first.
- When the wait has been long, ask the visitor if someone else in the firm might help.
- Some secretaries suggest a tour of the company for the first-time visitor to help pass the time.
- Another option is to offer a cup of coffee and some reading material.
- Do not ignore the visitor; keep the visitor posted on the boss's expected arrival time.

- Offer him a place to work or even a telephone to use. Chances are he will be glad to make use of this time interval.
- Some visitors like to engage in conversation. In that case, talk to the visitor even if other work has to wait a few minutes. Sometimes a little light chatter helps soothe anxiety.
- Stay calm and maintain your secretarial poise. The manner in which visitors are treated when waiting can greatly influence the outcome of a meeting. I know of one secretary who, according to her employer, is so lovely, charming and gracious to office visitors that the boss makes sure that certain "difficult to handle" clients wait in the reception room with the secretary. She unfailingly gets them in a good mind-set before being ushered into the boss's office—a real testimonial to a secretary with a lot of poise.
- Everyone is detained occasionally, but when delays become habitual, a hint to the boss could help. He may not be aware of the severity of the problem or just needs a little push to get to appointments on time.

Public Relations Liaison for the Office

Good PR (Public Relations) builds the image of any business. Today corporate executives are becoming more involved in community, educational, and service endeavors as financial supporters and advisers. As a result, company secretaries are also more involved in acting as the PR liaison. This may require dealing with the media, not always an easy job. It is a good idea to establish a working rapport with local newspaper editors, TV and radio networks, and members of organizations such as the Chamber of Commerce, Small Business Bureaus, and other business and professional organizations.

An official business card bearing your name and title is an easy way to introduce yourself and helps put a meeting with the media on an official basis.

If you are new at handling the media, here are some guidelines:

- Assign ONE person from your organization to deal with a news media contact. Two or more staffers calling the same newspaper can lead to conflict or confusion.
- Quickly establish personal contact with the right person at each newspaper, radio or television station in your area, i.e. medical reporter, listings editor, program director. Learn their style and what they expect so you can be ready for them at any time.
- Write everything down. Train your memory, but do not rely on it. Writing down specific instructions when taking directions, phone messages, and other incidentals relating to office duties is similar to making a grocery list. No matter how many times you have prepared a particular recipe, if anchovies are not on the list, the Caesar salad is going to lack a major ingredient.
- Meet deadlines. The media does not wait.
- Type news releases using the standard format.

  NOTE: See Appendix F for a sample press release.
- Be accurate in every statement. Double check dates, names (spellings), places and time before submitting information.
- Be brief, clear, and concise. Newspaper space and air time are costly.
- Be honest and impartial. Give credit where due. If the press release you are preparing concerns the accomplishments of several staff members, give credit to all. Do not emphasize one person's achievements just because that person is your supervisor.
- Do not be afraid to suggest something new to either your boss or the publicity department if you believe you have a newsworthy idea. Most media people welcome original features.

- As in your other dealings with people, businesslike. Never try to obtain publicity pressure of friendship or busine connections.
- Be appreciative of all space and air time giv your organization. A thank-you note or telephone call to the media person responsi for airing your news release will help get t next one placed.
- Be professional. Members of the press a always invited guests. Never ask them purchase tickets or pay admission to a function. Arrange a special "Press Table" large affairs.

The Mechanics of Preparing Press Releases

If you have never prepared a press relea familiarize yourself with the following standard forr preferred by the media:

- News releases should be typed or print double-spaced on 8 1/2 x 11 inch paper. Tv inch side margins allow the editor space write comments.
- Use company or organization letterhead a be sure the date is at the top. After the da move several vertical spaces and in the cen type "Contact Person." Name the person, a give a phone number. Usually the pers named is the one who can best answ questions from the media.
- Type FOR IMMEDIATE RELEASE either at left margin or centered a few lines beneath contact person and phone number. Sho you write a headline? Since most editors wr their own, a headline for a press release probably not necessary; however, place subject at the top of the release.
- Avoid slang, company jargon, and techni language. Use short, easy-to-understa

words. Newspaper English is dignified but vivid, simple but varied, ample but non-technical.

- Use short words, short sentences, and short paragraphs. Use action verbs and words that draw a picture.
- Paragraph, punctuate, and spell properly. Avoid abbreviations, adjectives, and wordiness. The release will probably be cut anyway.
- Keep the release date in mind so that the "today" and "yesterday" make sense in the article.
- If the release runs more than one page, end each page at the end of a paragraph and write "more" at the bottom. Copy is often divided and pages are given to different typesetters.
- At the end of the release put "end," or ### (three number symbols), or the number "30." Each signals the editor that you have finished your information.
- Allow plenty of time for a news release to reach the media in time for the release date. Delivery by hand is the best guarantee.
- Send news releases to all the newspapers in town and to as many reporters and editors at those papers as the news release warrants.
- File a copy of the news release for comparison with the article as printed in the paper. After comparing, note what was deleted or changed. This will help you write better releases in the future.

From the Word Processor to the Camera

If you have a picture to send along, the release will probably attract more attention. As the old saying goes "One picture is worth. . .ten thousand words." Some companies keep a camera on hand for taking on-the-spot pictures as needed. Who knows when t secretary might be called from the word p cessor to take a couple of pictures for a pr release? When preparing photographs for t press, do the following:

- Use black and white film for newspape newsletters, and other publications. Black a white glossies reproduce better in print. Pri of 5 x 7 inches are preferred.
- Reproduction is best when photos are clean smudges and fingerprints and contrast b ween light and dark areas is good.
- For interesting pictures, show key people action.
- Focus on the action. Eliminate extraneo background material.
- Write captions identifying people, place, da and event on the lower half of a sheet of pap or an adhesive label. Tape the caption to t back of the photo or attach it to the bottom the picture.
- Identify all persons correctly (from left right). Include names, titles, and organizatio
- Two or three individuals—not more th four—make the best photo compositions.
- Move in close when possible and concentr on facial expressions and human inter encounters.
- ''Before and after'' photos make a spec impact if they suit your copy.
- Experiment with the camera. Photograph t commonplace in an uncommon way: try hig low, or wide angle shots.

In your line of duty as a secretary, who knows, y might even discover a new talent and hobby a become a camera bug.

Handling Unscrupulous Callers

In addition to dealing with the media and handling scheduled visitors, the secretary must also cope with unofficial office vistors who simply appear. Though many office buildings post ''No Soliciting'' signs, unfortunately, they do not deter sales people, or callers trying to solicit confidential information about your company or callers with fraudulent intents.

The U.S. Labor Department recently warned employees about a new scam—thieves who pose as ''inspectors'' from OSHA (Occupational Safety and Health Administration) to scan offices for later fraud. The Labor Department advises that genuine OSHA inspectors carry credentials that legitimate inspectors readily present. They should have no objection to waiting while you verify their identity. Persons claiming to represent either federal, state, or local government agencies, and who wish to inspect your office for any reason, should be able to provide you with a telephone number so that you can check their claim. One call might save your office thousands of dollars in stolen items or information.

The National Office Products Association (NOPA) warns members and customers that questionable office and stationery supply firms have been the source of numerous inquiries and complaints over the past few years.

It is characteristic of these unscrupulous firms to change their names and addresses frequently, making it difficult to maintain accurate records of their operations.

These operators use several techniques to sell their products. One frequently-used tactic is the long distance sales pitch in which the caller claims to have a large surplus of merchandise in your geographic area because of a canceled order. The items are offered at a tremendous discount.

Other pitches include (1) claims that the owner died and left a large inventory that must be liquidated, (2) a free gift offer, (3) a statement that a friend or another business in the area (actual names are used) referred them to you, or (4) indications th they are affiliated with the government using such titles as "Department of" "Agency of."

NOPA suggests the following steps to protect yo firm from such schemes:

- Ask the caller to put all offers in writi including the brand name of the items, a pri list, and the full name, address, and pho number of the company. That is usually t last you will hear from a questionab company.
- Assign one staff member to approve all orde and offers.
- If you do receive unordered items, refu delivery if at all possible. Alert the purchasi department about potential problems.
- If the shipment was accepted, do not use a of the order. Write to the company advisi that, because you did not place an ord payment will not be made. Tell them to pi up the merchandise.
- Also remember, if merchandise you did n order is shipped, you are under no obligati to return or pay for it.
- Your best defense is to do business only wi recognized office supply and office machi and equipment dealers.
- A good reference source to read, if you wa to implement a "boiler room defense" is T Snodgrass' book, *Office Purchasing Guide.* S the appendix for book-ordering informatio
- For further information on how to gua against fraudulent deals or for a list of NO dealers in your area contact:

NATIONAL OFFICE PRODUCTS
ASSOCIATION
301 N FAIRFAX DRIVE
ALEXANDRIA VA 22314
Phone: (703) 549-9040

CHAPTER 10

Within the Office Environment

Happy families are all alike.

—*Leo Tolstoy*

Secretaries—The Human Factor in Office Systems

We hear quite a bit about the environment these days and are told that it is everybody's job to help improve it. The office environment does not consist of fields and trees; rather it consists of people relating to one another. Anything you can do to help improve relationships between individuals, outside or within your office, makes the office environment a more rewarding work place.

Regardless of how sophisticated and how computerized, the most important ingredient for a successful office operation continues to be the human factor. In *Megatrends,* John Naisbitt remarks, "The more high technology around us, the more the need for the human touch." The role of the secretary can certainly be pivitol in meeting the need for that human touch.

Though your computer may be programed to "talk" to callers, a computer cannot calm an irate client over the phone. Nor will there ever be a machine built that can exhibit the tact of a secretary who must deal with a finger-drumming client when the boss is running late.

Can a word processor or a computer keep a secret if everyone in the office knows the password? An executive can count on the confidentiality of the secretary. Machines break down, but the secretary is there from nine to five and often beyond.

The secretary is a self-starter—no floppy disk needed. Not only are secretaries responsible for the efficient and smooth flow of work in the office, but they must be creative and have a keen sense of the total operation of the organization.

As discussed earlier, the secretary has the savoir-faire to take over complex duties in a meticulous and exacting manner yet still keep a fast-moving pace in the office setting. In this setting, the secretary has an opportunity to set a congenial, cooperative tone for the entire office community.

As a professional, here is how you can accomplish this:

- Try to be pleasant to everyone—a difficult task, but one that pays off. When you pass along instructions from the boss, remember that they come from ABOVE you, not from you. The wrong approach can build a barrier between your supervisor and the rest of the office staff. Resentment can build up against you. Should the boss bark, "Where's that d. . . report from the Accounting Department?" do not relay the message in those same words. Be tactful; just say that the report is needed in a hurry. If your boss calls someone on the carpet, do not be unpleasant to that person yourself. Keep a neutral position.
- Be pleasant to office visitors. A pleasant manner not only helps vistors relax but also puts them in a good frame of mind to do business.
- Be impersonal. When someone says, "Good morning, how are you?" do not give an ache-by-ache account of your latest ills. Keep your private life private.
- Do not jump to conclusions. Think about this often-repeated situation. You are given a statistical report to type and proof in an hour, but you have just started on another lengthy document and are on page one with the executive office diskette in the word processor. Before you jump down someone's throat, find out why you were asked to do the job. Perhaps you were chosen as the only one who could handle it.

- Do not complain. A constant stream of complaints puts others in a bad mood too, and the office environment deteriorates. There are paths to take to eliminate a genuine grievance, so don't burden those who can do nothing about a gripe.

The professional secretary constantly relies on common sense and good judgment, human qualities essential to success on any job. A computer is only cooperative if programed correctly. The secretary comes already programed with the positve, cooperative attitude necessary to boost the morale of the entire office staff. Such attitudes can add to the total productivity of the office. Let's take a look a some of these professional attitudes:

Negative:	Positive:
"I really don't think it will work."	"Let's try it and see."
"It's impractical; let's just forget it."	"Let's consider it from every angle."
"Why get a new machine? I'm doing fine on this one?"	"Maybe I can increase my productivity with it."
"Suppose it doesn't work?"	"Can we do it on a trial basis?"
"The boss might not like it."	"I think I'll get the boss's opinion and suggestions."
"I knew it wouldn't work."	"Let's try a different approach."
"None of the others are doing it."	"We're more productive than the other offices."

The Role of Staff Confidante

Keeping confidential information away from outsiders can be difficult. An equal challenge can come from within an organization, especially if you find yourself in the role of staff confidante. Pressure from those curious for information can be particularly intense if you work for an elected official, or if you are secretary to the president, or chairman-of-the- board, or have a boss in a policy-making position. Having access to priviliged information exposes you to co-worker's hopes, dreams, and ambitions as well as their complaints, gripes, and dissatisfactions.

One secretary to a local elected official saw a good friendship go down the drain because a co-worker (supposedly a good friend) constantly quizzed her about upcoming zoning law changes. The co-worker's husband was involved in real estate dealings that involved zoning-laws.

The questioning of the secretary by the co-worker occurred at the office, at lunch, on social occasions, even phone calls at home. The situation deteriorated so much that the secretary wound up avoiding the co-worker.

The responsibility of being close to the "top brass" does not have to be a frustrating experience. The following suggestions should help keep priviliged information top secret while still keeping co-workers on your side:

- Do not betray confidences. The secretary with savvy is the secretary who can keep a secret.
- View your co-workers from the sidelines; do not try to be a watchdog. Observe fellow employees' work habits, personality traits and their work ethic. Familiarity with your co-worker's traits should make it easier to assess their complaints, inquiries, etc.
- Careful observation of fellow office workers can help resolve problems. For example, is the complaint from "Mr. Overworked" justified? Or would he have time to do his job properly if he quit making so many personal phone calls on company time? Is "Ms. Never-been-promoted" also the same worker who continues socializing way after the coffee break should have ended?
- Chronic complainers stand out. Every office has one or more. They are fairly easy to handle if you listen, remain noncommital, and tell them that you really do not know enough about the situation. If they persist, tell them you will be glad to investigate—this usually gives them satisfaction, without alienation.

- Maintain an "open door" policy. However, do not turn into the office martyr by overdoing it. Tactfully inform staff members that you have your job responsibilities to fulfill too. Inform them that their concerns may have to wait. A "waiting period" can lessen or even eliminate a co-worker's "urgent" problem.
- If you hear the same complaint from several staff members, consider this a warning signal. First investigate the matter yourself. Obtain unbiased facts from those in the know. If the problem proves to be serious enough, you should take it to your boss for his evaluation.
- If you decide to approach the boss, select a time that is convenient for him. Present a balanced, impartial report outlining what the problem is—try not to mention names.
- If your boss asks your opinion, be candid, honest, and sincere about your findings.

Remember secretaries, you wear many hats. Two important ones are being a good sounding board and having a good shoulder to cry on—so lend a shoulder and an ear, and remain the good office confidante.

Secretary and Boss—A Winning Team

Believe it or not, the one person in the organization that many secretaries find easiest to handle is the boss. There is no question that the secretary is the person the boss relies on the most. How often have I heard a business executive comment, "I will accept the promotion (or the transfer) on the condition that I can take my secretary with me." Whether the secretary is moving up with the same boss, having to adjust to a new boss, or is named the new boss, no ingredient will increase the office productivity more than the secretary and boss working as members of a team—truly a winning team.

Professional secretaries quickly learn what their bosses rely on them for most. For example, one may find it necessary to screen phone calls and visitors more closely for some executives than for others. Also many depend on their secretaries to answer all routine correspondence while others prefer to answer everything themselves.

The professional secretary is usually understanding and learns to see another's point of view. If the boss requests an unreasonable assignment in a limited time and then explodes when it isn't finished, stay calm. Not an easy task, but if you allow yourself to be upset, the job will take even longer. YOU know you are doing your best. You will also realize that there was poor planning on the part of your supervisor but that there are times when this happens.

As one secretary said, "Unpredictable days in my office are the norm. If I'm not working on some detailed business project, she has me help with her community or civic organization commitments. It isn't unusual to be interrupted in the middle of a corporate report that requires intense concentration to prepare a resolution for Cub Scout Troop 10. Flexibility and a sense of humor are MUSTS in working with my boss, and I've learned to have both." This is what working as a TEAM is all about.

Loyalty to your company and your boss is another sought-after attribute in the secretary. This, together with taking pride in one's job, makes the secretarial profession one of the finest. The secretary who continues to grow professionally by updating skills, taking pride in quality work, and supporting the boss at all times will continue to be a winner on the office team.

Adjusting to a New Boss

A new secretarial assignment could come at any time. You could be transferred to another department within the organization; your boss could retire, move, or be transferred; your company could merge with another, resulting in a complete reorganization.

Begin your new assignment by keeping past successes in mind. This will restore any self-confidence you may have lost due to changes, a new boss, or a return to the work force after a long absence.

- Be open-minded and receptive to change; accept new office routines as a challenge. Look at your job (new or old) as an opportunity to learn another skill and gain knowledge in a new area.

- One approach to a new assignment is to pretend that you have a brand new job. With a new job, there are new procedures to learn. Remember that new equipment requires new methods.
- Do not be afraid of your new boss; rather, learn from him.
- Above all, do not be shy about asking for help—even if you have to ask those to whom you used to give help. Do not step on toes, and keep in mind that you are not alone in getting used to a new situation.
- Find out exactly what procedures your new boss wants to pursue and FOLLOW THEM. You might, however, say, "Do you want me to continue doing this as I have been doing or do you prefer another way?" This might serve as a hint that there IS a better way. At any rate, give the boss the option of deciding how the office is to be run. (Even if the secretary ends up running it.)
- As you work with the new boss, be sure to find out which tasks and policies are considered priorities and adjust your schedule accordingly. Once you find out what he wants to achieve and how he intends to go about it, support him—one hundred percent. By doing so, your duties will probably broaden, and you will begin to enjoy your new boss as well as your new duties.
- ASK QUESTIONS. Ask about the overall operation of your company. You might even request a briefing on the company's objectives and ways you as a secretary can help in achieving them.
- Executives compliment their secretaries on taking the initiative, such as drafting routine correspondence or gathering information on a specific project in advance. Some bosses are grateful to be relieved of less urgent tasks.

Learn to second-guess your boss. Think like

management. Put yourself in your boss's shoes and anticipate his needs. If you can foresee future needs and solve problems before they occur, you are on your way to becoming part of management. You must keep in mind that your boss is also trying to prove himself in a demanding situation. With your help, you and your new boss will form a dynamic team.

Stress — Learning to Cope

Much has been written in the past few years about stress—what it is and how to handle it. One thing seems certain: everyone experiences stress at some time or another. For the secretary, innumerable situations can be stressful—an important decision must be made and there is no one available to ask for advice, several deadlines must be met simultaneously, or problems at home that get in the way at the office. Although these are examples of ''negative'' stress, let's consider the possibility that stress can also work in your favor in the form of a challenge or stimulant. Try these techniques; they may work for you.

- A positive attitude—Take an affirmative approach to your work. No matter how small the task or how much you dislike it, it has to be done. Give each job your complete attention and do it to the best of your ability. This alone will make you feel better when the work is completed.
- Organize—You will make the job easier in the long run. Collect work materials, read through directions, or perhaps prepare an outline. You will have a clearer idea of what you are trying to accomplish.
- Pace the work—Do not rush just to get it over. Stop at intervals and double check for accuracy. You may avoid the possibility of redoing an entire document or project.
- If you find tension building, leave the job for a while. Complete another task, and come back later. After a coffee break or a lunch break, you might have a more relaxed attitude toward the job.
- Learn to be adaptable. Just because you usually

prepare a sales report in the morning does not mean that you cannot do as rapid and accurate a job later in the day. TRY IT. Do not get upset when you are asked to postpone those transcripts and begin the day with a different job. Routines are meant to be broken.

- Try to develop a sense of humor. It is a great coping tool.
- Do not hesitate to express your concerns to your boss or co-workers. This can release pressure, and you might receive suggestions that will help lighten your work load.
- Evaluate your own traits, skills, and job expectations. It is possible you expect too much from yourself.

There are two ways of meeting difficulties; you alter the difficulties, or you alter yourself to meet them.
—Phyllis Bottome, English Novelist (1884-1963)

Criticism—You can Handle It

Everybody receives criticism at one time or another, either in personal or professional circumstances. Secretaries are no exception. In fact, some receive so much criticism from co-workers that it seems part of their job description.

Regardless how gently it is administered, criticism is never easy to accept. But criticism can have a positive effect. A positive attitude will not only make criticism easier to bear but also create stronger relationships and understanding among people. Here are some guidelines:

- Take your work, not yourself, seriously. It is important to be sensitive TO criticism; do not be sensitive ABOUT criticism. If the office wit likes to tease you because you could not get the document to paginate the first time, just smile, call the machine ''dumb,'' and keep trying. Do not let teasing upset you, rather let the office joker have a little fun. No harm done.
- Do not make excuses when criticized. Above all, do not blame someone else. This is a real cop-out, and your boss and co-workers will recognize it as such.

- Analyze the reason for the criticism and try to take steps to prevent that situation from recurring. This is the constructive approach.

A secretary I know had a bad habit of interrupting co-workers with questions and comments when they were on the telephone. Finally, when staff members called this to her attention, she was shocked. She had never realized how irritating her habit was to others. Now, when that same secretary sees others on the telephone, she stays as far away as she can. In fact, it has become a joke around the office; when the phone rings, she runs in the opposite direction.

- Do not be resentful and sulk when you have been criticized; such behavior only calls attention to your mistake and gives the appearance of sour grapes.
- Recognize that sometimes your boss simply gives vent to his or her own frustrations. Unfair? Yes, but this is not the time to mention it. Wait until the situation cools and then discuss the problem. The boss will very likely be in agreement with your analysis.
- Discuss an unpleasant situation calmly. By getting a problem off your chest, you will not only feel better but also gain the respect of your co-workers.
- Above all, do not turn around and criticize the one who criticized you.

The Negative Approach Isn't All Bad

Learn to say NO; it will be of more use to you than to be able to read Latin.

-Charles H. Spurgeon

Secretaries are prime targets for all kinds of requests that are not necessarily part of their job description—everything from typing a report for a co-worker's child to coordinating an office social event. As uncomfortable as it may be to say "no" to certain requests, it becomes a must at times. For some, saying "no" is easy, but for others it is difficult. Listed here are situations you may encounter and suggestions for a graceful ''NO.''

- When asked to type a report or letter for a staff person you do not work for directly, you might respond, ''I wish I had time, but I must get this report finished as soon as possible, and it is taking longer than I expected.'' Do not add, ''Please ask me later if there is anything I can do.'' You will surely get asked later, and it may be even more inconvenient.
- If you are the only one in the office who knows how to use the word processor or other piece of equipment, you are a prime target for being asked to show others how to use it. Even if one of your superiors asks, you will have to say, ''no'' at the outset or the situation could become chaotic, and you will never get your own work accomplished.
- When someone on the staff suggests a change or wants you to sign a petition, by all means, say what you think. ''I am not really sure I agree,'' or ''It is food for thought—I will think it over,'' or ''Did you consider other options?'' Usually such a response is enough to get your ''no'' answer across if that is your intention.
- Learn to say ''no'' in a straightforward, confident way.
- Avoid long explanations that sound like excuses and rationalizations. Provide enough reasons to make sure that your denial does not lose a friend. Keep in mind that a ''no'' can be used to achieve positive results— sometimes a ''no'' to an interruption is a ''yes'' to production.

Office Politics—It Does Exist

Maneuvering, buck-passing, back-stabbing, and buttering-up-the-boss goes on in business and industry as consistently as in politics. Many a secretary has watched these executive political campaigns unfold as candidates fight it out in the corporate arena on their way up the ladder of success.

When one executive's credibility is on the line and

another is seeking a promotion, the office political game reaches a peak; it can get pretty dirty. Secretaries learn not to mistake style for substance or rhetoric for fact and to cope with dog-eat-dog office scenarios. Secretaries have to be able to handle insecure or overly ambitious co-workers in these "games" that are, unfortunately, not a trivial pursuit.

It is not easy to stay above the fray when a co-worker is the favorite of top management and takes advantage of the situation. Favoritism can result when a staff member knows someone the boss would like to know, or when a co-worker is particularly charming, or perhaps the hardest of all to witness, when the worker is a relative. As hard as they are to excuse, such circumstances must be handled with caution and temporarily overlooked. If the favored person is incompetent, the problem will usually resolve itself because that staff member will not be able to produce. However, there are those who fall into the "Peter Principle" category. Heaven help them; they will need it.

Another distasteful situation is having to choose between your immediate boss and that boss's supervisor. The situation can get pretty touchy and should be avoided if possible. Some co-workers get caught up in trying to pick a group within the company with whom to ally themselves. A poor selection here can be tragic.

My best advice to you in an awkward situation is

- Refuse to ally yourself with any group—regardless of their power.
- Avoid being used by a co-worker who is engaged in a power struggle.
- Ignore criticism; remember, you can handle it.
- Maintain peer respect at all costs.

Finally, if you discover you like politics, take my advice and run for a political office and serve your community. Leave office politics alone.

Executive "Suite-Talk"

Besides having a front row seat for observing office politics, being privy to confidential information, and being one of the most valuable players on the office team, the secretary is usually the person most able to translate executive suite language into plain terms. In fact, the secretary knows only too well that ''suite'' talk is not always so sweet.

Who better understands than the secretary that the boss's memo saying, ''Please stop by my office at your earliest convenience,'' translates to ''Get in here FAST.'' Another expression heard in top management pow-wows is, ''Of course, if you turn it down, your future with the company will not be in jeopardy.'' The secretary's version of this is usually ''Take it or you get fired.''

Inexperienced female secretary Jones may not have learned yet that the boss on his way up does NOT mean a night out on the town when, at five o'clock, he asks, ''Miss Jones, do you have any plans for this evening?'' Smart Secretary Jones is quick to answer, ''Yes''; otherwise she will be working until the wee hours on a special company project for ''Mr. Ambitious.''

The secretary knows that when a sales represenative who just lost an important bid to a competitor is told by the boss, ''It's OK; we'll get the next one,'' the boss has probably already started interviewing to get a replacement for ''Mr. Lost-It.''

Using the same instinct, the experienced secretary knows ''Are you having problems at home? Perhaps I can help'' is a tactful reminder to keep personal problems out of the office.

Executive ''suite talk'' will continue to amuse and amaze clever secretaries as they see through it to their own translations.

When Illness Hits Your Office

When illness occurs, the tragedy affects the office family as well as the victim's own family.

Perhaps no one can be more comforting and helpful from a business standpoint than the secretary. For example, if the boss is a cancer victim and is undergoing radiation or chemotherapy treatments, the secretary can coordinate the treatments with a less-active business schedule. The secretary is also in a position to help the ill executive in several other ways.

- Do not cram too many activities in too short

a time span. If your boss dashes from one meeting or task to another every day, the boss will become physically fatigued and emotionally tense. Whenever you can, avoid scheduling irritating interviews or pressure appointments back to back. Give your boss a few minutes in between in order to collect thoughts and catch a breath. Do not give the boss too many tasks which concurrently demand attention. This leads to more fatigue and stress.

- Plan business trips carefully, especially those involving considerable distances. Keep in mind the time changes from coast to coast. Plan flights that coincide with time zones and the business day and that allow for rest time. Try to schedule trips early in the week when the boss is less tired.
- Schedule demanding or hectic appointments early rather than at the end of the day.
- Remind the boss of appointments several minutes before they take place. This allows time for collecting thoughts and gathering necessary information needed for the appointment. For meetings outside the office, allow the boss plenty of time to get to them without having to rush.
- Try to avoid as many business luncheons for your boss as possible. Food is hard to digest when a business deal is crucial.
- You may help by setting up a reminder system for taking medication. Possibly the physician has prescribed a special diet. Encourage your boss to stick to it. If the boss is married, you might check with the spouse for special instructions that the boss might not have mentioned.
- Let the boss relax twenty minutes or so after eating. Set aside simple tasks, such as signing letters or reading immediately after lunch. Hold off people or messages that might start up a hectic pace too soon.
- Handle as many routine tasks as possible or

direct them to someone else in the office. Although your boss may think that he alone can handle a particular problem, others can ease the work load.

- It is possible that a heart attack could occur in the office. The American Heart Association offers a free booklet listing symptoms and suggestions about what to do. I recommend a copy for every office.

The Secretary Deals With the Two-Martini Lunch Crowd

Many secretaries today are faced with handling the "two-martini" lunch gang. These are people who return to the office in a humorous, jovial, and often boisterous mood after a noontime break that frequently extends two hours. Not only do liquid lunches interfere with the work of those enjoying them, but the production of the entire office can slow down as a result.

Unfortunately, many secretaries work for supervisors who are the biggest offenders. The best way to handle this situation, in many cases, is to humor them. If your office has coffee, pretend that you were just on your way to get some and will be glad to bring the boss a cup.

One of the most important facets of a secretary's job is to cope with fluctuations in temperament. If you like your boss and the boss is basically a good guy or gal, I would try to make the best of the post-martini situation.

Continue to work as if everything is normal. However, if the voice is too loud and speech is slurred or incoherent, by all means try to keep the offender out of earshot of office visitors and off the telephone. If calls are ever to be screened, now is the time. Perhaps the door to the office of the noisemaker could be discreetly closed.

I was told by a former student that her boss yelled and dictated nasty letters when he had had one too many. Her remedy was to listen, transcribe the correspondence, and hold them for signing until the next day. Most of the letters ended up in the wastebasket—put there by the boss.

If you have a close friendly relationship with the

boss or co-worker and feel that the problem is serious, tactfully suggest professional help. Alcohol (and in some offices drugs) problems are very real in business and industry today and should be out in the open and dealt with.

One last word of advice, secretaries, if you are asked to join that special lunch group, by all means decline with a tactful, "Thanks but I have work to catch up on," or even "I am doing a little dieting." Think of the chaos that could arise in the office if all the secretaries joined the martini-lunch gang.

The Art of Delegating Authority

J. C. Penny, founder of the department store chain, once said, "One of the qualities I would certainly look for in an executive is whether he knows how to delegate properly. . . Another is their ability to make decisions effectively. These two personality lacks have contributed to executive failure more than any other lacks in know-how."

The secretary in a supervisory or managerial capacity will find it necessary to delegate certain duties to keep the office operating smoothly. The art of delegating authority is an acquired skill involving trial and error.

"Mr. Holdfast" was assigned to do the research for a bid on a large contract. He spent so much time doing mundane clerical work (instead of assigning it to another staff worker) that he had no time to do his own research. As a result, the project deadline was not met and his company lost the bid.

Those in management positions must learn quickly how to delegate authority in order to avoid frustrations, ulcers, and headaches. Whether you have been put in charge of a large project, asked to coordinate a fundraiser for the boss's favorite charity, assigned the holiday office party, or simply need to delegate some of your own office responsibilities, here are some helpful guidelines:

- First, evaluate the overall scope of the job including the final objective. Categorize jobs as routine, clerical, and decision-making. This will help you decide which staff members are suited to specific jobs.

- Motivate the people you have chosen by sharing your enthusiasm and expressing confidence in them. Bolster self-esteem by reassuring your associates of their worth. A positive attitude sets the stage for a positive outcome.
- Be sure everyone understands what he is to accomplish and monitor the job progress frequently, but inconspicuously.
- Once you have made a decision, relax and let the subordinate demonstrate independence and initiative. How would you feel if your boss gave you a job to do and then moved in and did it? No one likes a vote of "no confidence."
- Keep a watchful eye in the background. Final responsibility is still yours, so you want to keep on top of things at all times.

Delegating is like anything else, the more you practice it, the more adept you become. Delegate, Secretaries, DELEGATE.

How to Ask for a Raise

Are you assuming additional responsibilities, doing an exceptional job, and getting complimented for your work by other staff members as well as your boss? Do you feel it is time for a salary increase but do not quite know how to approach the subject? The time has long since passed when the subject of salary was hush-hush during a job interview or even when raise time rolls around. We all work for a salary. It is natural to appreciate the dignity of working if the salary is higher.

Often executives are so busy they forget about promises relating to incentive plans and periodic salary increases. Many times immediate supervisors are unaware of what their secretaries earn or when raise increases are due and may be pleased when the subject is brought to their attention. The bottom line is, if you have been promised a raise at a specific time and that time has come and gone, it is up to you to broach the subject. If you have the initiative for other jobs around the office, surely you can take the initiative in asking for a raise.

If the company handbook spells out policies and specifications for wage reviews and raises, familiarize yourself with them. If a policy does not exist, go to your immediate supervisor and ask about standard procedures for your organization. If the boss outlined raise increments for you earlier, and has not mentioned them since, a reminder will be welcomed. Often, a nudge is all that is needed.

Before evaluating your current salary status, take a look at your general working conditions, the amount of bureaucracy, the atmosphere, and most of all, your current fringe benefits. You might even divide the benefits program into two categories (1) Health and Security Provisions, and (2) Conveniences and Recreation. Here is a checklist of benefits:

Hospitalization
Life Insurance
Medical Insurance
Workman's Compensation
Disability Insurance
Dental Insurance
Educational Aid
Sick Leave
Maternity Leave
Day Care Centers

Holidays
Christmas Bonus
Credit Union
Lunchroom Facilities
Profit Sharing
Bereavement Leave
Vacation
Jury Duty Leave
Coffee Breaks
Parking
Company Recreational Facilities

How many of the above are you receiving? There may be others not listed.

Discuss your situation only with the person who can get action for you. Otherwise, you'll create misunderstandings and resentment. The one person who knows your value is probably your boss. Lines of communication between the boss and secretary should always be open. It never hurts to let your boss know that you enjoy your job and that you are interested in upgrading your rewards as well as your responsibilities. Your future and interest in the company and your ambitions for progress are usually good approaches to take. Maintain a professional attitude at any cost, and do not act hurt or insulted because you have not received a raise. The threat to ''walk'' if you do not get called undignified and beneath the professional secretary's principles.

Be genuinely interested in your boss's comments concerning your raise. Often, raises are denied because of the financial condition of the company. New firms getting started are struggling to make it, and the rewards to employees will come later. You deserve the right to ask for a raise if you think one is due. Ask with pride and politeness, and pray that you get it.

Part V

The Secretary Stays Well Informed

CHAPTER 11

Information—Sources and Resources

A little library growing larger every year, is an honorable part of a man's possessions. A library is not a luxury. It is one of the necessities of a full life.
—Henry Ward Beecher

Professional Reading

Automation continues to affect changes in the office environment to the extent that more reading is imperative if secretaries are to stay well informed and do their jobs more effectively. Because so much information is available, much of it highly technical, selection becomes a paramount concern. Professional publications for secretaries, newsletters, magazines, updated reference manuals and many others deserve attention. In addition, it is advisable to read broader-based literature relating to your business or industry.

Reference Sources for the Office

No office should be without a reference library even if it is as modest as a single shelf in your book case. Listed below are just a few of the reference materials that secretaries may find helpful.

- Dictionary (one of the new collegiate editions)
- Office Procedures Manual for the Company
- Current Reference Manual for Secretaries
- Users' Manuals (keep near the equipment)
- Thesaurus
- Shorthand Dictionary
- Hyphenated Word Dictionary
- Typing Style Manual (word processors do not know all the rules)

- Almanac (historic, political, economic, geographic, and social data)
- Atlas (especially for the office with extensive operations over a wide territory)
- Shipping and Postal Guides
- Post Office Directory. Lists post offices (1) by states with ZIP Codes, (2) alphabetically, (3) by countries and military installations with APO addresses
- Current telephone directories—one near each phone if possible.
- Travel Guides for airlines, hotels/motels, and car rentals
- Credit and financial information sources
- *Office Purchasing Guide,* by Tod. J. Snodgrass Guidelines to buying supplies, printing, furniture and machines. See Appendix for book ordering information.
- Metric conversion information
- Company literature
- *"The Secretary's Friend"* newsletter (distributed free by some office supply dealers.) For further information write: Buck Morton & Associates, 1370 Chain Bridge Rd., McLean, VA 22101.

Suggestions to Improve Your Reading Rate

Most of us are so busy these days that we do not have a lot of time left over to read for relaxation much less for professional reasons. The only solution is to do more skimming, scanning, and selecting in order to stay well informed. Here are a few good speed-reading hints:

- Do not read word-by-word.
- To preview long magazine and newspaper articles, business reports and non-fiction books, read the first couple of paragraphs through; then read only the first sentence of the remaining paragraphs. Finish up by reading the entire last paragraph or two, which usually summarizes.

- To get a general idea, skim for a few key words in each line.
- Skim if you have read the material before.
- Concentrate on seeing several words at once. Look at groups of words instead of single words.
- If you are unable to use these techniques successfully, consider enrolling in an evening or weekend speed-reading course.

Most of us would like to read at a faster rate—fast enough to read all the things we want to read, instead of only the things we have to read.

Newsletters—a Growing Pool of Information

One source of information used increasingly to update personnel on the latest technology and trends is the newsletter. Besides being on the reading end, secretaries may also find themselves on the preparation end of newsletters that are distributed by their own offices.

If you find yourself with the job of newsletter preparation for your company, begin with the following guidelines:

- Define the purpose of the newsletter
  - To promote company morale
  - To promote public relations/advertising
  - To provide information to help promote better job performance
- Determine your readers
  - Staff members of your organization
  - Clients, business associates
- Keep readers in mind when preparing content
  - Newsletter material should be timely, informative, and relevant. Example: A computer company newsletter should keep its readers informed about special software programs and their applications and uses, troubleshooting techniques, and how to remedy problems with them, new hardware available, new technologies, etc.

- Production of the newsletter
  - Are both graphics (typesetting/typing, photos, illustrations, photos, logos, etc.) and printing to be produced "in house"?
  - Are just graphics to be produced "in house," with the printing to be done by an outside professional printer?
  - Are both graphics and printing to be done by an outside professional printer/graphics house?
- Suggestions for "in house" preparation
  - Use generous margins, single space individual articles, double space between paragraphs.
  - Keep paragraphs and articles brief and to the point.
  - Use boldface and larger print for titles, headings, key words, and phrases.
  - If your firm has graphics software available, it is helpful in making attractive sketches and charts.
- Newsletter Specifications
  - Print on 8 1/2 X 11 inch paper: It is easy to handle and easy to mail.
  - Print on both sides of the sheet.
- Determine method of distribution
  - Courier or hand delivered
  - U. S. Mail
  - Other

There are many simple ways of improving newsletters. In addition to inferior writing, inaccuracies, and errors in grammar and punctuation, watch out for other flaws that weaken a newsletter.

- Copy reduced in size too much, making it hard to read.
- Poor reproduction. If typing is dim or dirty, or if the reproduction process is inefficient, copy will look slip-shod.

- Poorly conceived layout. Arrangement of copy, artwork and white space should be tastefully balanced.
- Inconsistent headline style. Example: Boldfacing some headlines and not others or using too wide a variety of fonts.
- Poor handling of article continuation—hard to find, located inappropriately, no reference to continuation location.
- Unjustified right margins. Do not be afraid to divide a word if it will improve the appearance of the copy.
- Incomplete publication information—name, address, editor, etc.
- Amateurish, inappropriate, or overcrowded artwork.
- Unprofessional general effect—unclear, "cutesy" or too elementary.

Mailing Lists—Another Phenomenon

With the rapid growth in mass mailing, specialized direct mail marketing services with the ability to process and mail over 200 million direct mail pieces a year are another phenomena facing today's secretary. Third-Class mailings, which require permits registered with the United States Postal Service, are over a million a year with many permit holders maintaining several mailing lists.

Being able to expedite such voluminous mailouts is another breakthrough that the expanded capacity of the computer has made possible. A mailing list can be tailored to the needs of your business and can reach virtually any audience, from all the corporate lawyers in Tunisia to all the gemologists in Mexico City, by checking specific categories of information on a computer form, such as geography, industry, size, range, status, etc.

If your office is in the process of developing a direct mail campaign for the first time, you may want to keep these facts in mind:

- If you are compiling your own mailing list and have exhausted all your sources, a list broker or one of the direct mail marketing services are good sources for further entries. You may obtain more information from the Direct Mail Marketing Association.

- Advance planning is advisable as lists are prepared. All data that goes on the list should be complete, such as ZIP Codes and telephone numbers. Time will be saved if all data is stored on the computer at the same time.
- If you are compiling your list "in house," a computer consultant can supply information about database software that will make your direct mail campaign easier to manage.
- There are four basic formats to choose from for your mailout:
  (1) Floppy disks from which you print via your own computer. These are good for volume and repeated mailings.
  (2) Computer-printed labels prepared for you—also good for large-volume mailouts.
  (3) Pre-Printed Cheshire Labels. These are printed on plain bond paper and are inexpensive.
  (4) Pressure sensitive mailing labels. These are pregummed and can be affixed by hand or machine.
- Mailing lists should be purged several times a year (at least twice). In doing so, weed out duplicate names and data on the list. The match code system, which uses letters or symbols that coincide with other designated letters or symbols, is commonly used to automatically weed out unwanted data.

Special Direct Mail Terms to add to your Vocabulary

Bar Code The bottom 5/8 inch of a business reply card or letter size envelope that is reserved for USPS (United States Postal Service) information.

Blow Out A card-sized insert placed in a magazine or catalog to attract attention by falling out as the reader thumbs through the pages.

Demographics The economic and social makeup of a group of individuals, communities, businesses or institutions.

Lettershop A business specializing in direct mail services and related functions such as advertising. Some services provided are the preparation of mailing lists, collating, and addressing.

Match Code Uses letters/symbols that coincide with other designated letters/symbols to sort, retrieve and compare data. In a (direct) mail campaign, a match code could, for instance, tell you the number of responses from a particular ZIP code.

Nixies Refers to names on a mailing list that are returned by the post office as undeliverable.

Nth Name A method using every tenth name of a mailing list to obtain a cross-sampling of the list.

Purging A process by which duplicate names are removed from different mailing lists and/or addresses and names are updated.

SIC Standard Industrial Classification, system that classifies businesses by services or products.

Sampling A test of pulling power of a mailing list, mailing pieces, or promotional offer.

Split Run A test using statistically identical mailing lists to test the appeal of two or more promotional offers.

Voluntary Review Postal inspection of sample reply pieces is not normally required prior to distribution by permit holders. However, permit holders are encouraged to submit such materials to their local postmaster for review prior to printing and distribution.

The U.S. Postal Service—A Cost-Effective Friend

You may never be involved in large volume mailings or newsletters, but most secretaries cannot avoid decisions about mailing services and therefore should be familiar with the U.S. Postal Service's procedures and services, which change frequently. If properly used, these services can be cost-effective in expediting your mail.

Mail collection boxes can be used to advantage if you are familiar with collection procedures. In fact, in some instances mail will move faster if you use the collection box rather than taking your mail to the post office at the end of the day. Boxes have different markings, indicating the type of mail that should be deposited in a particular box and the frequency of service. In some areas, boxes are identified with the words **Local Delivery.**

Familiarize yourself with the following information on the classes of mail:

- **First-Class Mail** may be sent at a reduced rate of postage (PRESORT) if it consists of at least 500 pieces and is presorted by ZIP Code according to specific postal regulations. An annual fee is required—consult your post office. Check from time to time to make sure the required number of pieces has not changed.

- **Second-Class** (publication) **Mail** includes newspapers and magazines issued at least four times a year. The publisher must obtain a second-class permit from the post office for a special rate, which varies depending on the frequency of publication; proportion of advertising to content; and whether or not the publication is mailed to an address within the zone of publication.

- **Third-Class** (advertising) **Mail** consists of circulars, booklets, catalogs, and other printed materials not requiring First-Class mail service. It also includes merchandise, farm products and keys. Each mailing piece must weigh less than 16 ounces. There are two sub-categories: single piece rate and bulk rate. Bulk rate requires a Bulk Rate permit and is applicable to mailings of identical pieces separately addressed to different addresses in quantities of not less than 200 pieces or 50 pounds. Mailing pieces must be ZIP Coded, presorted, and bundled (lengthwise and crosswise) with twine strong enough to withstand handling. Rubber bands may also be used with letter-sized mail.

In case you have ever wondered what those little colored dots on the envelopes of some mailed pieces signify, they are color-coded self-adhesive labels used to identify the type of bundle. The dots indicate the following:

- **Direct Bundle** - Red dot with letter **D.** Use when there are at least ten pieces of mail for the same five-digit ZIP code. If no label is available, mark the top piece Direct.

  JOSEPH DEER
  D 1234 FOREST ST
  DOWNTOWN ME 04512

- **Mixed City Bundle** - Yellow Dot with letter **C.** Use when at least ten pieces of mail remain for a multi-ZIP coded city. If no label is available, mark the top piece with **Mixed City.**

  WILLIAM DOE
  C 567 DAYTON BLVD
  DAYTON OH 44569

- **Three-Digit Bundle** - Green Dot with number **3.** Use when there are at least ten pieces remaining and you have prepared all possible ''Direct'' and ''Mixed City'' bundles. If no label is available, stamp the top envelope **Mixed SCF.**

  MR BRIAN POST
  3 1358 FIRST AVE
  CAMDEN PA 19123

- **Mixed State Bundle** - Orange Dot with the letter **S.** Use if ten or more pieces remain after all of the above bundles have been prepared for that state. Mark **State** on top piece if no label is available.

MARY WHITEHOUSE
S 78 DOMINION WAY
ALBANY NY 12035

- **Mixed States Bundle** - If the remaining pieces in the mailing have not fallen into any of the above categories, face them one way and tie. Insert a piece of paper marked **Mixed States** under the twine or rubber band covering the address on the top piece of this bundle. Carefully follow the postal instructions for your Third Class mailouts, and you will expedite your mailing.

- **Fourth-Class** (Parcel Post) Packages weighing a maximum of 70 pounds and measuring up to 108 inches in length and girth combined can be mailed anywhere in the United States by Fourth Class Mail. Your local post office can advise you on the best methods of mailing parcels of all types—books, records, materials for the blind, diskettes, catalogs, and international mailings.

- **Express Mail** is now available which guarantees next-day delivery (use ''B'' label for post office to addressee) or next-business-day arrival for pick-up at the post office by addressee (use ''A'' label for post office to post office). To use this service you should know these facts:
  - Express Mail must be received at the post office by 5 p.m. Weekend deadlines may vary.
  - Anything that is not dangerous, perishable, or restricted, up to 70 pounds, may be mailed.
  - The U.S. Postal Service guarantees to get the mail to the destination Express Mail Post Office by 10 a.m. the next business day. Since the mail will be delivered to the post office, the person or company to whom the mail is addressed should be notified by the sender that the mail is ''on the way'' so that someone can pick it up at the post office.

Currently, approximately 1000 cities are served by Express Mail.

- For an additional fee, the U.S. Postal Service guarantees delivery direct to the addressee by 3 p.m. on the day the mail arrives at the destination Express Mail Post Office—365 days a year.
- If the Express Mail is not delivered as guaranteed, the sender can receive a full refund of the postage by presenting the original mailing receipt and, if possible, the addressee's delivery receipt showing the failure. The sender must complete an application for the refund within 60 days from the date of the mailing at the originating post office.

Other Special Postal Services

- **Business Reply Mail** consists of specially printed business reply cards, envelopes, cartons, or labels for use in returning mail without prepayment of postage. A permit is required. The form must be submitted to the post office where the mail will be returned, except as follows: If business reply material is distributed from a central office to be returned to branches or dealers in other cities, one permit obtained from the post office where the central office is located may be used to cover all the business reply mail. All post offices where mail is returned must be provided with a copy of the paid receipt (FORM 3544) by the addressee showing date and place of payment. For information concerning permit fees, collection of postage, and business reply mail format, contact your local post office.
- **Mailgram** service enables you to send a message to virtually any address in the continental United States and Canada for the next business day. Simply call WESTERN UNION's toll-free number and dictate your message to the operator. The message is transmitted electronically to the post office

serving the recipient and is delivered by a regular carrier the next business day. Take time zones into consideration. To insure next-day delivery have your message in before 7 p.m. destination time.

- **Registered Mail** is a high-security service available for all items mailed at the First-Class or priority rate of postage. It is the safest way to send valuable and irreplaceable articles. Checks, money, jewelry, and stocks and bonds are some of the items that should be sent "Registered." Leases, mortgages, wills and other vital business records are also often sent this way. Registry fees include proof of delivery as well as mailing and indemnity protection up to $25,000. For an additional nominal fee, a return receipt showing delivery information is available.
- **Certified Mail,** like registered mail, is available for all articles mailed at the First-Class rate of postage. Any first-class mail that has no dollar value of its own (such as a letter, or important notice) may be certified. The sender receives a receipt and a record of delivery. Certified mail provides no insurance, however.
- **Special Delivery** service is available for all classes of mail. It is available at offices served by city carriers and within a one-mile radius of any post office. Special Delivery receives preferential treatment in processing and transportation and fast delivery at the destination post office. It is also delivered on Sundays and holidays. Fees vary according to the class of service and weight of the article. Special delivery can be deposited at the same points as First-Class (mailboxes, etc.) but it is recommended that you make your deposit at postal facilities to insure separation from regular mail and to get the best service.
- **Special Handling,** providing expeditious handling in dispatch and transportation for Third-class and Fourth-Class mail is available

for a nominal fee based on weight and class of mail.

- For mailing computer diskettes, you may choose First-Class, Special Delivery or Special Handling. Regardless of the class chosen, it is advisable to secure the diskette safely in a box or mailer pouch and write DO NOT X-RAY on it. The diskette will then be hand canceled, not sent through a scanning machine.

- **Postal Money Orders,** a safe and convenient way to send money through the mail, may be purchased at all post offices in amounts up to $700 nationwide. Should your money order be lost or stolen, it will be replaced (SAVE your receipt). Money orders can be redeemed at many banks, stores and business as well as at all post offices.
- **International Money Orders** can be purchased in amounts up to $700 at most large post offices and selected smaller post offices.

In order for mail to be sorted and dispatched quickly and efficiently by a high speed scanner (Optical Character Recognition), the post office makes these recommendations:

- Address typewritten or printed in all capital letters. Single space and omit punctuation. Use the nine-digit ZIP if it has been assigned.
- Avoid using several stamps of small denominations when you can use a larger denomination. Do not crowd the address area.
- Carefully check postage on mail going outside the United States. Rates are usually higher than domestic rates and often depend upon the destination. (Non-denominated stamps such as the A, B, C, and D stamps, marked domestic, may not be used.)
- Many businesses use postal meters, eliminating the need for supplies of postage stamps in various denominations. Postage is paid by a printed meter stamp.

Metric... When?

In addition to asking when we will switch to metric measurements in this country, you may also want to know why it is on the reference book list for your office. In 1968, Congress allotted $1.3 million to research the possibility of "going metric." At its conclusion, the study recommended a ten-year period of gradual conversion.

In the Metric Conversion Act of 1975, the federal government articulated a national policy of coordinating increased use of the metric system in the U.S. emphasizing that conversion is voluntary on the part of American firms.

The European Common Market has fixed 1989 as the date after which imported products must be labeled in metric units. If the U.S. goes metric, when and how does it affect your job as a secretary?

The secretary may not be directly involved in the actual conversion, but there are metric style rules for typing numbers that should be used in typing reports, correspondence, etc. These are listed here:

- Use a space instead of a comma to separate three digits to the left of the decimal point.

Examples:			
	0.2234	is shown as	0.223 4
	1,886	is shown as	1 886
	38,569	is shown as	38 569
	446,925	is shown as	446 925
	3,458,269	is shown as	3 458 269

- Use lowercase letters to begin the name of a unit (except at the beginning of a sentence.) NOTE: The word "Celsius" is capitalized.

  Examples: We used a liter of distilled water.
  Where is the meter stick?
  The temperature is 28° Celsius today.

- Certain measurements for area and volume are expressed with a superscripted number when printed. These measurements may, however, be expressed as abbreviations in typewritten material.

Examples:	Preferred	Acceptable
	cm^2	sq cm
	m^2	sq m

- Singular and plural abbreviations are the same.

Examples:	Correct	Wrong
	978 cm	978 cms
	400 kg	400 kgs
	38 cc	38 ccs

- Abbreviations or words may be used to express a unit of measurement.

  NOTE: Always leave a blank space between the last digit of the number and the abbreviation.

  Examples: 210 cc or 210 cubic centimeters
  44 ml or 44 milliliters
  22 mg or 22 milligrams

- A period should not follow a metric abbreviation, except at the end of a sentence.

  Examples: The flask contained 300 ml of solution.
  They added 5 g of FeS.

- A diagonal (/) is used to indicate the division of units expressed as compound symbols.

  Examples: m/s (meters per second)
  k/h (kilometers per hour)

- A sentence is never started with an abbreviation.
- Place zeros to the left of the decimal if there are no other digits to the left.

Examples:	Correct	Wrong
	0.08	.08
	0.984	.984

- If metric terms are written out, use figures or words. Use figures only with abbreviations.

  Examples:

Terms Written Out	Terms Abbreviated
nine (or) 9 meters	9 m
fifty (or) 50 grams	50 g
two (or) 2 centimeters	2 cm

Is Another Keyboard On The Horizon?

The well-informed secretary of today knows that a new type of keyboard has been developed and may come into common use. Though the Dvorak keyboard may come as news to many typists and nontypists alike, its origins began in the 1930's when August Dvorak, a professor and efficiency expert at the University of Washington patented the device. According to Michael Kleper, Rochester Institute of Technology, it is being used today with "quiet success in a number of installations across the country." According to a fact sheet issued by Dvorak International Federation (DIF), founded in 1978 to promote the Dvorak as an innovative simplified alternative keyboard, acceptance of the Dvorak has intensified in the past five years for these reasons:

- Electronic keyboards have eliminated the possibility of jammed keys for typists who work fast.
- There is growing emphasis on worker productivity and comfort. Dvorak users are up to 40 percent more productive and report less fatigue on the job.
- Advances in word processors and computers mean keyboards can be easily converted to Dvorak by inserting a new program or program chip and changing the caps on the keys.
- Popularity of home and business computers makes typing and keyboard skills essential for millions of new users, including efficiency-conscious managers.

The American National Standards Institute, Inc. (ANSI) approved the Dvorak keyboard as a standard in 1982. Major keyboard companies like Key Tronics have introduced a Dvorak add-on keyboard for the IBM PC. Digital Equipment Corp. of Massachusetts will soon offer the Dvorak layout on their VT-100 terminal, Apple Computer already offers the Dvorak on the Apple IIC, and Wang is making the Dvorak available on its OIS and VS and on professional computers. Other computers can be converted with the proper software.

The biggest obstacle to Dvorak conversion is training and retraining. Microcomputers offer the brightest hope because they provide keyboards which can easily be switched between the universal and Dvorak layouts. For further information write:

VIRGINIA RUSSELL PRESIDENT
DVORAK INTERNATIONAL FEDERATION
11 PEARL STREET
BRANDON VT 05733

Keyboard Comparison

DVORAK

QWERTY

Professional Secretaries International (PSI)

The Certified Professional Secretary (CPS®) rating offers a significant, measurable, and attainable goal for career-oriented secretaries who want to be identified as exceptional. To qualify for the CPS® rating candidates must pass a two-day, six-part examination administered twice a year in May and November by the Institute for Certifying Secretaries. Six significant sections (reprinted by permission of PSI) of the CPS® examination include:

- **Behavioral Science in Business** – This part of the examination tests the principles of human relations and your understanding of self, peers, subordinates, and superiors. It focuses on the fundamentals of needs and motivations, conflict, problem-solving techniques, essentials of supervision and communication, leadership styles, and understanding of the informal organization.
- **Business Law** – This section measures (1) the secretary's knowledge of the principles of business law (not merely definitions) as they operate in the work-a-day world, and (2) knowledge of the content and implications of governmental controls on business. Understanding the historical setting in which controls developed should be learned rather than simply memorizing names and dates.
- **Economics and Management** – Emphasis is placed on understanding concepts underlying United States/Canadian/Jamaican business operations. Division of focus is 35% economics and 65% management.
- **Accounting** – Part IV measures (1) knowledge of the elements of the accounting cycle; (2) ability to analyze financial statement accounts; (3) ability to perform arithmetical operations associated with accounting, computing interest and discounts; and (4) ability to summarize and interpret financial data.
- **Office Administration and Communication** – Half of this test section consists of office administration covering subject matters unique

to the secretary's position such as executive travel, office management, records management, and reprographics. The other half consists of written business communications, editing, abstracting, and preparing communications in final format.

- **Office Technology** - This section covers the secretary's responsibilities in data processing, communications media, advances in office management, technological applications, records management technology, and office systems.

To receive further information, order CPS® study materials, obtain a membership application for PSI, or subscribe to their magazine, ''The Secretary,'' write to:

PROFESSIONAL SECRETARIES
INTERNATIONAL
301 E ARMOUR BLVD
KANSAS CITY MO 64111-1299

CHAPTER 12

Quick and Easy Brush-Up—Spelling, Punctuation and Grammar

A few strong instincts, and a few plain rules.

—William Wordsworth

Every secretary should know the rules of spelling, grammar, punctuation, and usage. Consistent day-to-day application of these rules marks the true professional.

Spelling—The Sandtrap of the Secretary

A secretary must be able to spell correctly since he or she takes dictation, transcribes, and proofreads the vast majority of the words produced in the office.

Today secretaries can side-step some spelling problems in documents prepared on a word processor or computer equipped with a spelling checker. However, not every secretary enjoys this luxury, and the spell checker cannot help you with proper usage of a word. Spelling rules are a help despite their many exceptions.

- **Is it ei or ie ?**
  - If the sound is a long **ē,** as in the word **bē,** then **i** before **e** except after **c** is the rule everyone remembers: chief, field, grief, niece, relief, wield, yield.
  - After **c**: ceiling, deceive, conceit, receive.

    Exceptions: protein, caffeine, seize, financier
  - If the sound is other than a long **e,** the word is usually spelled **ei**: foreign, heir, neighbor, forfeit, height, weight

Exceptions: friend, sieve, mischief.

- **Final silent e:**

  If a word ends in a consonant and a silent **e,** drop the **e** before adding a suffix beginning with a vowel. Keep the final **e** if the suffix begins with a consonant.

  have + ing = having care + ful = careful
  like + able = likable
  place + ment = placement
  notice + ing = noticing

  Exception: If the word ends in **ce** or **ge** and you are adding a suffix beginning with **a** or **o,** keep the final **e.**

  courage + **ous** = courageous
  notice + **able** = noticeable
  knowledge + **able** = knowledgeable.

- **Sede, Ceed, or Cede?**

  Some of the most bothersome and frequently misspelled words are those containing the sound of "seed." Learn three basic principles concerning these, and you will conquer all "seed" words.

  - **Sede:** Only one word and its derivatives are spelled with **sede.** This word is SUPERSEDE. Derivatives are SUPERSEDING and SUPERSEDED.
  - **Ceed:** Only three words and their derivatives are spelled with **ceed.** They are PROCEED, EXCEED, and SUCCEED.
  - **Cede:** If a word has the sound of "seed" and is not one of the above four, the word and its derivatives are spelled with **cede.** Most "seed" words fall into this category. Examples are precede, intercede, secede, acceding, concede, antecedent.

- **Prefixes:**

  Never add or drop letters when adding prefixes to words.

  dis + appoint = disappoint
  un + necessary = unnecessary

- **Suffixes ness and ly:**

  The word does not change when adding these two suffixes.

  plain + ly = plainly
  plain + ness = plainness
  mean + ly = meanly
  mean + ness = meanness

  Exception: If the word ends in **y,** you usually change the **y** to **i** before adding **ness** or **ly.**

  empty + ly = emptily
  empty + ness = emptiness
  heavy + ly = heavily
  heavy + ness = heaviness

  However, one syllable adjectives ending in **y** normally follow the first rule.

  shy + ly = shyly   shy + ness =shyness

- **Plural Nouns—add s or es ?**
  - Add **s** to most nouns to form the plural.
  - To words that end in **s, x, z, ch,** or **sh,** add **es** to form the plural.
  - If a noun ends in **y,** change the **y** to **i** and add **es.**
  - Nouns ending in **o** and preceded by a consonant add **es** to form the plural.

    Exceptions: solos, pianos, sopranos, altos, silos
  - Nouns ending in **f** or **fe** usually change the **f** to **v** and add **es;** however, some add only an **s** and others form the plural either way. Check your dictionary when in doubt.

NOUNS - ves	**NOUNS - s or ves**
half/halves	dwarf/dwarfs or dwarves
knife/knives	scarf/scarfs or scarves
shelf/shelves	

NOUNS - s

safe/safes	roof/roofs	chief/chiefs
proof/proofs	gulf/gulfs	

(and most other nouns)

- These words follow no regular rule in forming the plural.

woman/women	trout/trout	ox/oxen
child/children	tooth/teeth	man/men
goose/geese	sheep/sheep	deer/deer
moose/moose	mouse/mice	foot/feet

- **One Word or Two ?**

  - These words are always spelled as one word:

everybody	anything	nobody
someone	cannot	nevertheless
already	altogether	classroom

  - These words are always spelled as two words:

even though	all together	inasmuch as
in order	in fact	any one
some day	some time	no one
a lot		

NOTE: Several ''all'' and ''al'' words cause confusion—but not if you know their meanings.

all ready = ready	already = previously
all together = together	altogether = entirely
all ways = all (the) ways	always = invariably
all right = all (is) right	[alright/incorrect spelling]

- **Words Frequently Misspelled**

absence	appreciable	convenient	extraordinary
accept	arguing	criticism	familiarize
accidentally	attendance	decision	February
accommodate	bankruptcy	definite	financial
accuracy	beginning	departure	forty
accustomed	believable	desirable	fourth
achievement	benefited	difference	gauge
acknowledgment	business	disastrous	grateful
across	calendar	eligible	grievance
advisable	canceled	embarrassed	height
agreeable	cancellation	endeavor	hindrance
among	category	enforceable	illegible
analyze	chargeable	equally	immediately
apologize	coming	equipped	incidentally
apparent	committee	exaggerate	interfere
appearance	competitive	exceed	jeopardize
appointment	conscientious	explanation	judgment

knowledge
legible
leniency
loose
lose
maintain
manageable
mediocre
merchandise
miscellaneous
monotonous
mortgage
necessary
negotiable
nevertheless
ninety
ninth
noticeable
nuisance
occasion
occurred
occurrence
omitted
ordinarily
pamphlet
parallel
possession
preferred
prejudice
privilege
promissory
pursuing
questionnaire
receive
recommend
reference
remittance
salable
separate
significant
shipping
similar
stationary
stationery
strength
strictly
suppose
surprise
tariff
their
transferred
unanimous
undoubtedly
unnecessary
usable
valuable
whether
wholly

Punctuation and Mechanics

Punctuation is unique to written communication. When we speak, our tone of voice groups our words and places emphasis where we want it. When we write, we insert special marks to indicate groupings and to place emphasis.

Mechanics refers to capitalization, abbreviations, and use of numbers in writing.

Punctuation

Secretaries are familiar with standard punctuation marks—period, comma, question mark, apostrophe, etc.—but some punctuation marks cause confusion and raise doubts about what is correct. When does one use a dash or a hyphen? What are the rules for capitalization of the titles of government officials? How does one express a fraction?

- **A DASH (—) of PUNCTUATION**

The dash (made by striking two hyphens on the alpha-numeric keyboard) shows a break in thought, makes an emphatic point, or sums up. Here are the basic rules for the correct use of the DASH:

- Break in thought

> The miniature dictionary—only 3 inches by 5 inches—was not easy to use.

She accepted her loss emotionally—but with dignity.

- Emphasis of a single word

  The secretary seeks one thing—perfection—above all else.

- Summary

  Decision-making, keyboarding, transcribing, composing, proofreading—all are skills in word processing.

- Interruption in a sentence

  If only I could remember what I named the document—but who can expect to remember all text names?

- Apposition

  Mr. Brown—president of our company—is supportive of the entire staff.

- Restatement

  The patient was suffering an incredible amount of pain—much more pain than the doctors had seen before with this disease.

- Hesitation

  The committee had to read several resumes—well, rather a large stack—before making a decision.

The dash can also replace commas, colons, semi-colons, and parentheses when you wish to give greater emphasis to the idea following the dash. An idea may also be set off by two dashes.

Instead of:

Good language skills, namely spelling, punctuation, and grammar, are necessary to be successful at using word processors.

Try this:

Good language skills—spelling, punctuation, and grammar— are necessary to be successful at using word processors.

• HYPHENS — A DIFFERENT DASH of CONFUSION

Winston Churchill once remarked, ''One must regard the hyphen as a blemish to be avoided whenever possible.'' While many secretaries will agree with this sentiment, the hyphen is a useful part of our punctuation system when used properly.

The hyphen has two functions. It forms compound elements and divides words at the end of a line. Rules for dividing words at the ends of lines are fairly straightforward:

- Always use a hyphen when you must divide a word at the end of a line.
- Always divide the word at a syllable break.
- Never divide one syllable words (used, edge, plate.)
- Never isolate a single-letter syllable (o/pinion, a/dapt.)
- If a word already contains a hyphen, break the word only at the hyphen (semi-illiterate to semi-   illiterate.)
- Never hyphenate the last word of a paragraph or the last word on a page.
- Never divide numerals, acronyms, or contractions if they come at the end of a line.

With the increased use of the word processor, there has been some relaxation of the rules that govern dividing words at the end of the line. However, for clarity, certain rules should be maintained if you are forced to divide a date, proper name, or address.

- November 23, 1982 (Divide between the day and year.)
  November 23, / 1982
- Mr. Claiborne Morton (Divide between the first and last name; keep the first name with the title.)
  Mr. Claiborne / Morton

- John White M.D. (Divide between first and last name; keep M.D. with last name.)
  John / White M.D.
- Cleveland OH 44100 (Divide between city and state; keep ZIP with the state.)
  Cleveland / OH 44100

The rules for forming compound words or other compound elements are not as cut and dried. Much depends on the writer's meaning and contemporary usage. Use of the hyphen is declining— being used only when needed for clarity or emphasis. The well informed secretary should nevertheless know the basic rules for the use of the hyphen:

- Prefixes and Suffixes - Hyphenate most words that begin with ex-, self-, pseudo-,.

  ex-wife, self-limiting, pseudo-psychology.

  Hyphenate words that end with -odd, -elect

  forty-odd, president-elect
- Double and Triple Consonants - Hyphenate to avoid awkward double or triple consonants.

  hull-less, bell-like, co-opt, semi-illiterate
- Clarity - To avoid ambiguous words or words whose meaning could be misinterpreted, hyphenate.

re-cover (cover again)	recover (repossess)
re-cite (cite again)	recite (narrate)
a new-car dealer	a new car-dealer
a dirty-window washer	a dirty window-washer
- Compound Numbers:

  (1) Compound numbers from 21 to 99 are hyphenated.

  seventy-nine, twenty-one, ninety-nine

  (2) Numerals before words forming compound adjectives are hyphenated.

  six-year-old child, four-cylinder motor, 30-minute speech

(3) Spelled-out fractional numbers are hyphenated unless one of the numbers already contains a hyphen.

two-thirds, one-half, four and six-sevenths; but, twenty-four hundredths, five thirty-fourths

- Compound modifiers - Hyphenate words which form compound modifiers when the modifier precedes a noun. Do not hyphenate when the compound comes after the noun.

He is a well-known man.
That man is well known.
The staff received an across-the-board raise.
The staff received a raise across the board.

- The Suspended Hyphen - In a series of compounds all of which have the same second element, use a 'suspended hyphen' after the first element, space once after the hyphen and before the next word.

two- ,three- , and four-story buildings
5- , 10- , and 12-digit numbers
long- and short-term loans

In all cases, the wise secretary will check the word(s) in question in a dictionary since there are so many exceptions and rule changes. The best policy is to be consistent. Unless there is a required style for your office, you will find it simpler to eliminate as many hyphens as possible.

- **THAT BIG LITTLE APOSTROPHE**

The little apostrophe is another punctuation mark that causes problems—when to use it and where to put it?

- Use it to indicate omissions of one or more letters

do not	don't	it is	it's
he will	he'll	could have	could've

- Use it to show possession

  (1) singular noun—add an (**'s**):

  office's desk's

  (2) plural noun—add (') only to nouns ending in **s**:

  offices' desks'

  (3) plural noun—add (**'s**) to plural nouns that do not end in **s**:

  men's children's

  (4) Singular possessive of compound noun:

  sister-in-law's car

  (5) Plural possessive of a compound noun. Add an apostrophe (') if the plural form ends in **s**:

  chairpersons' decision
  housekeepers' duties

  Add (**'s**) if the plural compound form does not end in **s**:

  editors-in-chief's work
  mothers-in-law's house

  (6) Possessives showing separate possession. Add the appropriate sign of possession to each owner:

  Anne's and Jane's lockers
  cats' and dogs' feeding dishes

  (7) Possessives showing joint ownership. Add the sign of possession to the final name alone if all owners are identified by name:

  Anne and Jane's car
  mothers and daughters' clothes

  Add the sign of possession to each name if at least one owner is identified by a pronoun. Use the possessive form of the pronoun:

  John's and my car
  stockholder's and his decision

Mechanics

Getting It Together with Numbers

Accounting reports, annual reports to stock holders, production proposals—all require number processing. Therefore it behooves a secretary to know the accepted ways to express numbers. To allow for a uniform format, some traditional number usages have become more flexible with the advent of word processors and their automatic wraparound and margin justification features.

- **General Guidelines**
  - Spell numbers from one to ten except when used with numbers above ten. This applies to exact and approximate numbers. Consistency is desirable. Keep numbers in a sentence or group in the same style. But spell out a number that begins a sentence, regardless of the numbers that follow in the same sentence.

    The supply order included 6 ring binders, 12 boxes of computer paper, and 14 printer ribbons.

    Please send us five copies of your latest newsletter.

    Twenty-five diskettes were ruined by spilled coffee; 11 were saved.
  - When two numbers are used together, spell out the shorter (in keystrokes) of the two.

    The accounting department needs 50 one-page ledger sheets.
  - Numbers preceded by nouns are generally expressed in figures.

    The article appeared on page 4, section 3 of Volume 10, Number 9 of *The Secretary's Friend* newsletter.

    NOTE: An arabic numeral follows the word ''Volume'' even if the publication uses a Roman numeral in its masthead.
  - When two numbers appear together in a sentence and both are in figures (or words), separate them with a comma.

    By 1990, 990 words per second being printed from the laser office printer will not be uncommon.

- **Ages of Individuals**

  Ages frequently appear in hospital and insurance forms as well as legal documents. The following guides apply:

  - Express ages in figures when they are significant to a technical report—they are easier to read.

    Policyholders, ages 25 to 35, are eligible for special premiums.

  - In general and formal documents, ages are written out.

    The woman is in her early eighties.

  - When age is stated in years, months, and days, write the age in figures; commas are not necessary.

    The president will be 64 years 11 months and 29 days on his retirement day.

- **Addresses**

  - Spell out street names of less than ten; write them in figures if they are over ten. To avoid confusion, use a hyphen with a space before and after it when the house number and street number are both given in figures.

    My office is at 901 Fifth Avenue; my showroom is at 13 W. 42nd Street.

    Did he say the correct address is 430 - 14th Street?

  - The only number that is ever spelled out for a building or house number is the number "one."

    They plan to move from One Park Avenue to 1915 Sixth Street.

- **Amounts of Money**

  - Amounts of money are usually expressed in figures, and even sums of money are typed without the decimal and cipher.

    $10 $33 $2.37 $45.06

    NOTE: Round numbers in large amounts of money such as three million dollars may be written as "$3 million."

  - Spell out indefinite numbers and amounts of money.

    Several million dollars
    A few thousand yards

- For amounts under a dollar, use figures and the word ''cents.''

  This machine can be repaired with 80 cents worth of parts.

- Do not use the dollar sign and decimal in amounts under a dollar unless used in a sentence with related dollar amounts.

  The economy desk folder for the new secretary cost $3.50; its pad of paper, $.99; clip to hold paper, $1.75; and stick-on label, $.59

- The symbol ¢ is used in technical and statistical matter containing price quotations.

  Yesterday's wholesale prices for food were as follows: a can of soup, 65¢; a candy bar, 20¢; and a loaf of bread, 75¢.

• **Business Anniversaries**

- Rules vary for expressing company anniversaries and special events. A general style is to spell out numbers if they require emphasis or are more than one word.

  The 125th anniversary celebration took much planning on the part of the office staff.

  NOTE: For formal writing, ''One hundred twenty-fifth'' would be preferred.

• **Dates**

- When the day follows the month, expess it in cardinal numbers (21, 23, 30).

  April 30, 19-- December 23, 19--

- If the day precedes the month or is used alone, use ordinal figures (1st, 2nd, 3rd, 4th. etc.) or ordinal words (first, second, twelfth, twenty-eighth).

  The workshop for secretaries begins on the 23rd of April and runs through the 28th.

- Military style and certain foreign nations express the date by day first, month, and year. This style is also used for the Modern Simplified letter and in some government office. (No comma is used.)

  15 April 19-- 30 December 19--

- The current trend is to omit commas around the year when it follows the month alone.

  The records for June 1983 (or June, 1983) have been charged out to Ms. Jones.

- **Decades and Centuries**
  - In most styles—formal, general, or technical—decades and centuries are spelled out. If B.C. is used, it follows the year; if A.D. is used, it precedes the year unless it is used with the word "century."

    Twenty-first century

    Women of the eighties

    The Battle of Hastings was fought in A.D. 1066.

    The Battle of Hastings was fought in the 11th century A.D.

    Julius Caesar lived from 100 to 44 B.C.

  - If the century is used, the following style is preferred:

    in the 1990s 1980s technology

  - There are a few ways centuries and decades may be written as contractions; these include graduation and historical years.

    the class of '49
    '76 Bicentennial Celebration

- **Fractions**
  - Spell out isolated fractions in a sentence unless they are part of a mixed number or are used in a series with other fractions. Mixed numbers are usually written in figures except at the beginning of a sentence.

    Nearly one-third of the filing is completed.

    I hate to add 7/8, 1 1/4, 2/3, and 1/9.

    This generation of computers is 5 1/4 times more powerful than earlier ones.

  - Hyphens in fractions can be tricky. When fractions are spelled out, the numerator and denominator should be connected by a hyphen unless one element already contains a hyphen. Common fractions used as nouns may be written without a hyphen. Fractions used as modifiers are hyphenated.

Seven-eighths five thirty-seconds

One fourth of the office staff attended the lecture.

A two-thirds majority of the members voted to adjourn the meeting.

- Do not use words or suffixes as part of the denominator or a fraction.

Wrong:	9/300ths	45/32nds	6/8ths of an inch
Right:	9/300	45/32	6/8 inch

- A guiding rule is that if a sentence requires the use of an "of" phrase after the fraction, spell out the fraction.

  We still have time for another cup of coffee although three-quarters of the break is over.

- **Legal Documents**
  - In legal documents such as bank notes, wills, real estate contracts, etc., numbers appear in both figures and words.

    The principal of ten thousand dollars ($10,000) shall be paid in seventy-five (75) monthly installments.

- **Percentages**
  - The percent symbol is used only in special forms such as invoices and other technical documents. Express percentages in other documents in figures and spell out the word "percent."

    Discount: 2% within 15 days; 1% within 30 days

    They will give a discount of 10 percent if we pay within five days.

  - In a range or series of percentages, the word "percent" follows the last figure only. The % symbol, if used, must follow each figure.

    Prices range from 20 to 30 percent on all damaged goods.

    Prices range from 20% to 30% on all damaged goods.

  - Fractional percentages may be expressed as follows:

    One-half of 1 percent (or) .05 percent

- **Time**
  - Use figures with a.m. and p.m. Do not use a.m./p.m. unless figures are used.

    The boss's plane arrives at National Airport at 11:30 a.m.

    The boss's plane arrives in the morning instead of the evening.
    (Not: in the a.m. instead of the p.m.)

    NOTE: Type a.m. and p.m. in small letters without spaces.
  - Do not use a.m./p.m. with o'clock.

    He will be here by six o'clock. (Not: six o'clock p.m.)
  - Noon and midnight are acceptable, but when used with other times in the same sentence, be consistent by using the number 12 with noon and midnight.

    The second staff comes in at midnight.
    The nurse worked from 4 p.m. to 12 midnight
- **Scores**
  - Scores of sporting events, votes, etc. are preferrably written in figures as they are easier to read.

    5 to 1 between 10,000-10,500 votes
- **Special Symbols**
  - Use figures with symbols and abbreviations.

    #3 15% 46¢ $44 144 sq.ft. 8 in.
  - In a range of numbers, repeat symbols but not words.

    17%-25% $15-$30
    17-25 percent fifteen to thirty dollars
- **Arabic Figures and Equivalent Roman Numerals**

1	I	11	XI	30	XXX	400	CCCC
2	II	12	XII	40	XL	500	D
3	III	13	XIII	50	L	600	DC
4	IV	14	XIV	60	LX	700	DCC
5	V	15	XV	70	LXX	800	DCCC
6	VI	16	XVI	80	LXXX	900	CM
7	VII	17	XVII	90	XC	1000	M
8	VIII	18	XVIII	100	C	2000	MM
9	IX	19	XIX	200	CC	5000	$\overline{V}$*
10	X	20	XX	300	CCC	10000	$\overline{X}$*

*NOTE: A line over a numeral multiplies the value by 1,000: thus $\overline{X}$ = 10,000; $\overline{L}$ = 50,000; $\overline{C}$ = 100,000; $\overline{D}$ = 500,000; $\overline{DLIX}$ = 559,000.

- Other general rules in Roman Numeral are as follows:
  (1) Repeating a letter repeats its value — XX = 20; CCC = 300.
  (2) A letter placed after one of greater value adds thereto — VI = 6; DC = 600.
  (3) A letter placed before one of greater value subtracts therefrom — IV = 4; XLIX = 49

To Shift or Not To Shift

The use of capital letters is a convention that helps us emphasize or show the importance of certain words. Unfortunately capitalization is not always as simple as it seems. Rules that govern proper usage and help avoid unnecessary capitalization follow:

- Capitalize official titles preceding personal names.

  I would like to introduce Senator Richard White.
  The senator from South Carolina will arrive soon.
  I do not believe the president of the company, John Jones, will be here.

- Do not capitalize occupational titles when they precede or follow personal names.

  We liked the courtroom manner of Ed Walton, attorney.
  Dr. Jacobs, dean of Center College, will speak.

  However, when the occupational title is a specific job title: I think Editor Fred Freedman does an excellent job.

  NOTE: Some companies capitalize some or all titles of company officials. Always follow the practice used by your employer and respect the preference of others regarding their own names and titles.

- Capitalize titles of specific courses, but not references to general academic subject areas except languages.

The company wishes that all employees t the course, Human Relations in the Offi during their first year of employment.

The company advises that all employ during their first year take a course deali with interpersonal relations.

- Academic degrees are generally not capitali when used with the word **degree,** but **deg** is capitalized when used with the name of individual.

  Are you going to try for a master's degr
  Professor Jones, Ph.D. was my favo instructor at Warbash College.

- Titles of international, national, and st government officials are capitalized wl written before, following, or in place o specific person's name. These titles are capitalized when they refer to an entire cl of officials.

  The ambassador from Peru arrived in to yesterday.
  William Mitchell, State Representative, vo for the bill.

  The candidates for president must appea all voters.

- Capitalize the names of countries a international organizations as well as st county, city, and local bodies and the agen within them.

The United Nations	Departmen Commerce
The Reagan Administration	The Virgini Legislature

- Capitalize the titles of acts, bills, laws, treaties. Do not capitalize the short form u in place of the full name.

  Public Law 56—987
  The Panama Canal Treaty
  The Constitution of the United States
  Monroe Doctrine; but, the doctrine

- Specific names of products are alw capitalized; the product itself is not capitali unless it becomes part of the brand nam

The boss ordered a Lanier transcriber.
My son will eat only Heinz Catsup.

- Do not capitalize the words sun, moon, or earth unless together with the capitalized names of other celestial bodies (constellations, planets, stars) that are capitalized.

  The moon is in its last quarter.
  The planets Venus and Earth are second and third in order out from the Sun.

- Compass directions are capitalized when they refer to specific regions or when the direction is part of a specific name. These words are not capitalized when they merely refer to a general location or direction.

  I was born and raised in the Northwest.
  I was booked on Flight 10 on Eastern Airlines.
  Turn north on I—95 to get to Washington, D.C.

- Always capitalize the words Northerner, Westerner, Southerner, and Midwesterner.
- Such words as northern, eastern, southern, are capitalized when they refer to people in a specific region or to their political, social, and cultural activities rather than a general location.

  I like Southern hospitality.
  The western tip of the island was covered with pine trees.

- Capitalize the names of all institutions such as churches, libraries, schools, hospitals, synagogues, colleges, and universities.

  School of Medicine Library of Congress
  Department of Psychology
  Holy Cross Hospital

- Capitalize the important words in legal citations.

  People v. Jones, 35, VA. 60. 83—98 (1983)

  In law documents, many introductory words are in all capital letters:

  IN WITNESS WHEREOF, the parties...
  THEREFORE, BE IT RESOLVED, that the...

- Titles of complete published works—such as books, magazines, pamphlets, newspapers, and plays—are underscored, italicized or typed in all capital letters. This also applies to titles of motion pictures, long musical compositions, paintings, sculptures and other complete works of art.

  Titles of poems, songs and television or radio programs are enclosed in quotation marks.

Grammatically Speaking

Grammatical constructions give pause to many people, secretaries included. Who or whom? Will or shall? Each or every? Either or and neither nor. A secretary should include a good English grammar book among the reference volumes on the desk. Good places to buy a grammar guide are college bookstores. Abridged handbooks for introductory composition courses serve most needs. For a brief review, take a look at the following rules.

- **WHO or WHOM?**

  Although the use of **who** in place of **whom** has become generally accepted in spoken English— "**Who** are you voting for?"—the well-informed secretary avoids its misuse in business correspondence. **Who** is the subject form and **whom** is the objective for of this relative pronoun. If in doubt, replace who/whom with the appropriate personal pronoun. If you can substitute he/she/they, use **who.** If the personal pronoun him/her/ them fits, use **whom.**

	(Who/whom) did they elect?
Reverse to:	They did elect him.
Correct form:	Whom did they elect?

  When the relative pronoun is buried in a sentence, you must still determine whether it functions as a subject or an object.

  There were questions about (who/whom) was taking the mail to the post office.

Reverse to:	He was taking the mail.
Correct form:	There were questions about who was taking the mail to the post office.
	John knew (who/whom) we planned to offer the job to before the meeting began.
Reverse to:	We planned to offer the job to him.
Correct form:	John knew whom we planned to offer the job to before the meeting began.

- **WHICH or THAT?**

That introduces only restrictive clauses. Do not use commas to set off a restrictive clause from the rest of the sentence. **Which** may begin either restrictive or nonrestrictive clauses, although many writers prefer to use **which** only in nonrestrictive clauses. Now you are asking, ''How do I determine a restrictive from a nonrestrictive clause?''

A restrictive clause is necessary to the basic meaning of the sentence or clause in which it appears.

A job that requires a lot of overtime is not a good one for someone who wants to maintain an active social life.

A nonrestrictive clause merely gives additional information to the reader but is not necessary to the basic meaning of the sentence or clause in which it appears.

The job, which required frequent traveling, paid very well.

NOTE: Remember that **who/whom/whose** refer to people, **which** refers to animals or inanimate objects, and **that** can refer to either people or things.

- **THESE and THOSE for THIS and THAT**

Misuse of **these** and **those** for **this** and **that** is due to the misconception of singular and plural.

RULE: Use **this** or **that** before **kind** or **sort** even if the following noun is plural. **Kind** and **sort** are singular.

Right: We know nothing about that kind of products.

Wrong: We know nothing about those kind of products.

Right: We do not handle this sort of account.

Wrong: We do not handle these sort of account.

If **kinds** or **sorts** is used, **these** or **those** is proper.

- **EACH and EVERY** (Everyone- Everybody, etc.)

Again, misunderstanding singular or plural causes mistakes with the use of these pronouns with other pronouns and verbs.

Right: Everyone is expected to do his or her best.

Wrong: Everyone is expected to do their best.

Right: Each of the three executives was present.

Wrong: Each of the three executives were present.

- **SHALL or WILL?**

To express simple future use **shall** (or **should**) with the first person and **will** (or **would**) with the second or third person.

I shall look forward to hearing from you.
You will receive payment in a few days.
He will come to the office today.

To express determination or promise, use **will** (or **would**) in the first person and **shall** (or **should**) with the second or third person.

I will not record payment of this bill until Monday.
You shall certainly represent the company at the next meeting.
They should be forced to reconsider their position.

- **MISPLACED or DANGLING MODIFIERS**

  Efficient writers make their meaning clear to readers at once. Do not make your reader go over a sentence or passage several times to understand what you are trying to say. A misplaced modifier often obstructs understanding.

  - Misplaced modifiers can cause ambiguity in meaning.

    Confusing: I caught favorable glances from other office personnel dressed in my new fall outfit.

    Clarified: Dressed in my new fall outfit, I caught favorable glances from other office personnel.

  - Place your phrase and clause modifiers as close together as possible.

    Confusing: Ernest Hemingway's novels have been made into successful movies of his earlier period.

    Clarified: Ernest Hemingway's novels of his earlier period have been made into successful movies.

  - The subject of the modifying clause and the main clause must be the same to avoid the dreaded dangling participle.

    Confusing: While filing correspondence, the message came from the front office.

    Clarified: While filing correspondence, I received a message from the front office.

- **SUBJUNCTIVE MOOD**

  A frequent mistake is in the use of the verb in the subjunctive mood. The subjunctive expresses a wish, supposition, or condition contrary to fact. It takes a special form of the verb ''to be''; the form is ''were'' for all persons.

Examples:

I wish I WERE in Mexico.
He wishes he WERE sailing.
If she WERE elected to the Senate, she would always consider her constituents.

- **POSSESSIVE with the GERUND.**

Use the possessive case of a noun or pronoun before a gerund. A gerund is the ''ing'' form of a verb used as a noun. Examples:

John's leaving caused me much unhappiness.
I admire his taking time to explain the new system.
I shall appreciate your letting me know when you will finish.

- **POSITION of PREPOSITIONS.**

Winston Churchill said it. ''This is the sort of English up with which I will not put.'' Let it be said once again. It is ALL RIGHT to end a sentence with a preposition. Some style manuals still emphasize that you should never end a sentence with a preposition, but too many times this results in infinitely awkward constructions. Prepositions may precede their objects or they may follow.

Prepositions may often be moved. Consider the formality or informality of your writing and place prepositions where they fit best. Examples:

About what are you talking? (or) What are you talking about?

The restaurant in which we ate was very expensive (or) The restaurant which we ate in was very expensive.

However, if the sentence is awkward, leave the preposition at the end.

AWKWARD: A preposition is a word with which one may end a sentence.

BETTER: A preposition is a word one may end a sentence with.

- **ACTIVE and PASSIVE VOICE**

At some time or other, you have probably been told, "DO NOT use the passive voice." The usual reason given for this advice is that the passive voice is weaker than the active voice, and after all, who wants weak sentences. The student naturally comes to believe that there is something wrong with the passive voice. Not true. It is perfectly all right to use the passive voice. In fact, there are several instances when it is better to use the passive form of the verb.

But first, you may ask, how does a writer tell the active from the passive. In the active voice the subject acts. (The clerk filed the letters.) In the passive voice, the subject is acted upon. (The letters were filed by the clerk.) A simple way to tell the difference is to try to insert a phrase beginning with **by.** Examples:

ACTIVE: Someone ate all the chocolate donuts.

PASSIVE: The donuts were eaten **(by** someone.)

ACTIVE: Mr. Block asked his secretary to take dictation.

PASSIVE: Mr. Block's secretary was asked to take dictation.
Again you can insert a **by** phrase—"by Mr. Block."

NOTE: The passive voice also usually employs some form of the verb **to be.**

Do not feel guilty. There are times when the passive voice is the better choice, and if that is the case, use it:

- When the action is more important than the doer of the action

Snow mixed with sleet was predicted for tonight's rush hour.

- When the doer is unknown or indefinite.

  The noon flight was canceled and rescheduled for tomorrow.

  In this case, you do not know who canceled the flight, nor does it matter. The important information is its cancellation.

- When special emphasis is desired.

  Confidentiality for personnel files was of great importance to all staff members.

- Technical writing tends to use the passive to maintain an air of objectivity or detachment and to avoid the use of **I**. Instead of writing, "I cut and mounted the single-crystal electrode," a scientific writer would use the passive voice. "The single-crystal electrode was cut and mounted."

English Usage—Which Word and Why

As speakers and writers of English, we have a large and rich vocabulary to draw upon. But English contains many words that confuse. They look alike or sound alike or perhaps the meaning of a word is not precisely understood. Usage problems present both spelling and proofreading difficulties.

- **AFFECT or EFFECT.** Of all the words in the English language probably none cause as much confusion as **affect** and **effect.** Part of the confusion stems from the fact that both words can act as a noun or a verb. A secretary's best bet for distinguishing between them is to remember that **affect** is rarely used as a noun and **effect** is seldom used as a verb. If you are looking for a verb, chances are you want the word **affect.** It has four meanings all starting with **a**.

  Alter: That decision will affect our working hours.

  Assume: She affects that attitude to get attention.

  Adopt: They decided to affect the trend in styles.

  Act upon: Cold and heat affect the body.

However, when used as a noun, **affect** means feeling or emotion (used mainly in psychology.) For example:

Elations and depressions are extremes of affect.

Effect, on the other hand, means (1) ''result or outcome'' when used as a noun, or it may mean (2) ''influence or operative force.'' For example:

(1) Her words produced the desired effect.

(2) The result of the experiment had a far-reaching effect.

But the verb ''effect'' means ''to produce, accomplish, bring about or execute.'' For example: Try to effect a solution.
Occasionally you might run into a phrase in which both verbs make sense. The correct choice depends entirely upon the intended meaning. For example:

One act may affect (alter or act upon) both things.
One act may effect (bring about) both things.
He wants to effect (bring about) a law on pollution.He wants to affect (alter or act upon) a law on pollution.

- **BETWEEN and AMONG.** In standard usage, ''between'' refers to two persons or things; ''among'' refers to more than two persons or things. Examples:

  The choice now lies between John and Robert.
  There is a sharp contest going on among the members of the House of Representatives.

- **LESS and FEWER.** ''Less'' is usually used to denote quantities of things not measured as separate units. ''Fewer'' is used when referring to items that can be counted. Examples:

  I drank less tea yesterday than I usually do.
  I drank fewer cups of tea yesterday than I usually do.
  There are fewer people smoking on airplanes this year than last.

There is less smoking on airplanes this year than last.

- **DISINTERESTED or UNINTERESTED.** "Disinterested" means "unbiased" or "impartial." "Uninterested" means "indifferent" or "not interested." Examples:

  The manager listened to the proposal in a disinterested manner.
  The audience was uninterested in the speech.

- **EAGER or ANXIOUS.** Some dictionaries show these two words as synonyms. The careful writer will recognize that **eager** has a positive and favorable connotation whereas **anxious** has a negative and apprehensive connotation. Example:

  Jane was eager to start her new job; however, she was anxious about her ability to fulfill her new responsibilities.

In this next section, you will find many sound-alike or look-alike words that provide stumbling blocks to even the most conscientious proofreader.

- **ACCEPT.** To receive: We will accept your offer.

  EXCEPT. To exclude: Everyone except Mary went to lunch.

- **ADAPT.** To adjust: One must adapt oneself to a new job.

  ADEPT. Proficient: The new typists were very adept.

  ADOPT. To accept: The staff will adopt new guidelines for coffee breaks.

- **APPRAISE.** To evaluate: The auction house appraised the painting.

  APPRISE. To inform: I will apprise you of the meeting date next week.

- **ASCENT.** To climb, rise: The ascent up the mountain was difficult.

  ASSENT. Permission, approval: The committee gave its assent to the minutes of the last meeting.

- **COMPLEMENT.** Complete or make perfect: That hat complements your outfit.

  COMPLIMENT. Express admiration: The actress received compliments on her performance at the stage door.

- **CONSUL.** An official: Senor Ramirez is consul for his country.

  COUNCIL. An advisory group: The Council of Governments approved the new tax base.

  COUNSEL. To advise or express an opinion as to action: The attorney gave helpful counsel to his client. The attorney counselled his client.

- **CONTINUAL.** Often repeated: His continual absences were noted by his supervisor.

  CONTINUOUS. Uninterrupted: We have conducted a continuous advertising campaign for the last three months.

- **DISCREET.** Prudent, tactful: One must be discreet when entrusted with company secrets.

  DISCRETE. Separate, distinct: Each staff member must be treated as a discrete entity when considering salary increases.

- **FARTHER.** Refers to distance only: This car goes farther on a gallon of gas than I thought it would.

  FURTHER. Refers to time, quantity or degree: I read further in the book than I had planned.

- **PRECEDENCE.** Priority: When selecting students for this course, we gave precedence to seniors.

  PRECEDENT. Establishing rules and laws: Freedom to vote was established as a precedent in the United States.

- **RESPECTFULLY.** With regard for: I respectfully submit my resignation.

  RESPECTIVELY. In the order given: The files were numbered one through sixteen respectively.

CHAPTER 13

Secretarial Tips and Timesavers

Time is the least thing we have of.

—Ernest Hemingway

Over the years I have received many letters from secretaries who are eager to share ideas with others in their profession. In this section, you will find some of the shortcuts, advice and techniques that these secretaries have found helpful in making routine jobs easier. One of the best pieces of advice to come across my desk lately is the following:

> ''When meeting the challenge of new assignments, I found my best ally to be a positive attitude and a pleasant work personality. Many new and seemingly difficult situations can be mastered with a smile and a willingness to put forth your best effort.''
>
> —Margaret P. Gay, Secretary
> Interim Temporaries, Inc.
> Lancaster, Ohio — former student

Another universal piece of advice mentioned by many secretaries as well as executives is well stated by Patricia A. McCarthy, a training officer for a federal agency ''. . . a secretary, no matter what grade or salary, [should] project a professional image by wearing appropriate clothing (not necessarily expensive). Speaking from experience, I have seen one secretary promoted over another just because of her appearance.''

The function of any job is production and one of

the quickest ways to improve production is to find and USE short cuts. A few of these timesavers are listed.

- When mailing several sheets stapled together at the top, fold the top third first. Much of the bulkiness will ease out of the bottom.
- When requesting a document to be signed, always provide a pen—preferably one with black ink. Black ink copies better than other colors.
- Cover the entire label on a parcel post package with cellophane tape to keep it firmly in place and protect the address from getting smudged or damaged by the weather.
- Check to be sure you have the return address for all letters before throwing away their envelopes.
- Attach necessary information to an incoming letter (such as, ''Invitation conflicts with appointment in Chicago on same date,'') before passing it on to the boss.
- Use the stamp area on an envelope for notes. For example, dates may be lightly written in this area when correspondence or payments are prepared in advance and held for a specific mailing date. Or, if you have a mailout and the address has ''Mrs. John Doe'' on the envelope and you wish ''Mary'' to follow ''Dear'' in the salutation that has to be added to form letters, write ''Mary'' in small letters in the stamp area to remind you to use ''Mary.'' The stamp, of course, covers any such message.
- If you have a file that you frequently refer to and often make telephone calls in reference to, add that often called phone number to the file tab to save looking up the number each time.
- ''A quick and easy way to save time is to accumulate photocopying errands (and other necessary but not timely tasks) until you have several items requiring... attention, [they then] can all be done at the same time.'' — Nancy J. Kramer, Administrative Assistant to the President, BDM International, Inc.

- A loose-leaf binder is an efficient way to organize information referred to frequently, such as forms used in reports, names and addresses of salepersons, convention and seminar announcements, etc.
- Try to memorize names, addresses, and telephone numbers of persons with whom you have frequent correspondence.
- Highlighting - Start using a highlighter to point out dates, times, etc. in correspondence before you pass it to your boss. This technique not only saves rereading time but can also be a reminder. Your daily calendar can also be highlighted to call attention to specific jobs that might have priority for the day. Use different colored highlighters to pinpoint different items.
- Use cards of different colors for your telephone file or spin-wheel directory to help you find numbers faster. Code them—green for customers, blue for vendors, white for service repairmen, etc.
- Color-code diskettes by categories for easy reference. Diskettes themselves often come in different colors or feature colored labels.
- Color code anything you can think of in the office. Almost every office supply item these days comes in a variety of colors—paper clips, Post-it pads, index cards, etc.
- When grouping several sets of papers together with paper clips, place clips at least one-half inch apart to avoid tangling.
- Keep your yearly office calendar on your computer; in this way you can quickly make changes and print out an updated copy.
- To conserve ink-pad ink, turn the pad upside down at the end of the day. The next morning the pad will be like new.
- It is easy to slide index inserts into cellophane tabs without bending them if you place a small piece of cardboard—same size as insert—

behind each insert. Slide the two in together, then remove the cardboard.

- When you leave a message on an answering machine, remember to give your area code if the call is long distance. Many calls never get returned because an area code was not given.
- When you receive a memo from someone in your own organization, first make a copy, and then type your reply right on the memo. This saves typing time and paper and reminds the sender of the message sent. Highlight your reply with an accent marker to make it stand out.
- When two people in an organization send a letter or memo together, the word processing center can include two complimentary closings instead of one so that each person's name and title follows the closing. If the modified block style format is used, put one closing at the left margin and the other at the center. Example:

Yours truly,	Yours truly, (may be omitted)
John S. Doe	Jane K. Kool
John S. Doe, Vice President	Jane K. Kool, Sales Rep.

If the block style is used and the letter is short, one name and title can be placed under the other with only one complimentary closing. Leave three (3) blank lines between the first and the second to allow for signing. Example:

Yours truly,

John S. Doe

John. S. Doe, Vice President

Jane K. Kool

Jane K. Kool, Sales Rep.

- If you mention your company's name in a document, always print it in boldface. This is one of many ways that you can be creative and make documents more attractive, individualized, and effective with the use of the word processor. (Refer to your instruction manual for suggestions and shortcuts for performing specific functions.)

- Handling diskettes properly can save time by keeping them in good condition.
  - Always place the diskette in its protective jacket after use.
  - Never touch diskettes through the window slots where the magnetic surface of the diskette is exposed.
  - Because diskettes are sensitive to extremes in temperature, keep them out of direct sunlight and away from other sources of heat. Store them at temperatures ranging from 40 to 125 degrees Fahrenheit.
  - Always use a felt tip pen when writing on envelope labels to avoid damaging the diskette inside.
- If a one-page form letter mailout requires manual folding, bring the bottom of the letter to an appropriate line of text in the letter to make the overlap come out even. Your folding will go faster if you use the same line in every letter.
- Avoid "office romances"; otherwise office productivity can suffer. As one secretary advised, "If you find yourself involved in an office romance, keep it as quiet as possible. Don't gossip about it among co-workers. Many such encounters often wind up with someone getting hurt. Avoid an office romance and you'll be a lot better off."
- Many professional secretaries visit office supply stores often to find out about new products and supplies that offer easier and more efficient ways to handle routine office tasks.

SECRETARIES, STAY WELL INFORMED.

In conclusion, I would like to share something from a former student of mine:

''Out of curiosity I asked my boss, 'What skills or personal traits do you find the most important in your secretary?' His answer to me was, 'I don't have a secretary, I have an associate.' I took that as quite a compliment and feel that is the answer most secretaries should strive for. I have worked for --------- for seven years as his Administrative Assistant for Finance and wear a number of hats working for him. He has given me the freedom to grow in my job by letting me exercise my own initiative and take on additional responsibility, and in turn he has gained an 'associate' who can cover for him in almost all areas of his job.''

-Catherine W. Foy
Assistant Secretary and Administrative Assistant for Finance - Systems Planning Corporation

That, Secretaries, is what being a professional secretary is all about. You, THE SECRETARY, are the real FRIEND—THE FRIEND OF BUSINESS, INDUSTRY, AND GOVERNMENT.

BUSINESS ''BABBLE''— Do Not Let It Intimidate YOU!

Computer language can be as baffling and bewildering as landing in a foreign country. Even the simplest words take on ominous new meanings in computer language; for example, the screen becomes the VDT (video display terminal) or CRT (cathode ray tube). My first advice to you in adjusting to this new technical language is, do not be intimidated. Lots of people are learning along with you. Secondly, do not get angry; GET EVEN. Join the jargon bandwagon. But watch out for acronyms, words formed from the first letters of words contained in a phrase or name; i.e., EDP for electronic data processing. *The Secretary's Friend* provides you with the translation of some of the ''techno- babble'' used in word processing.

Access To locate the desired data.

Adjust A control on some word processors that allows the operator to add or delete text and to reset margins.

Alpha Characters consisting of letters of the Roman alphabet; no numbers.

Alphanumeric A set of characters which usually includes letters, digits, punctuation marks, and special symbols, such as an asterisk (*).

ANSI American National Standards Institute which serves as a national clearinghouse and supervises standards within the computer/information processing industry in the United States.

Appending Documents The word processor composes a document from various paragraphs stored on a disk. This is also referred to as document assembly, building blocks, and document creation.

Applications Program The software that tells the computer how to do word processing, data processing, mail list sorting, etc. An example is *WordStar,* a software package to be used on a computer for word processing when you do not have a standalone system.

Archive A procedure which transfers text from the on-line disk to an off-line storage disk.

Arrow Keys The set of four directional keys that move the cursor on the display screen without erasing text.

Auxiliary Storage Supplementary storage areas that hold data outside the memory of the computer.

Background/ Foreground The ability of a machine to perform one function, such as printing out a document, while the operator works on a different document. Some standalone word processors with outlying attachments called *slaves* or *foxes* allow two operators to be keyboarding at the same time.

Backspace Key Moves the cursor from right to left across the screen to erase characters. On many dedicated word processors, the backspace key is located at the upper right-hand corner of the standard keyboard.

Backup Extra copies of documents, programs or equipment for use in the event the original is damaged or destroyed.

Bar Code An information coding system in which input is represented by bars of varying widths and positions.

Baud Rate The speed at which information is sent between computers.

Bidirectional Having the ability to move in two different directions; usually applied to printers which operate faster because of this capability.

Binary Digit Either the characters 0 or 1; abbreviated "bit."

Block A group of words, etc. regarded as a unit because they are stored in adjacent memory locations; data stored as a unit.

Boldface Characters or words that are printed darker by repeatedly printing over them.

Boot Up	Start up, as in turning on the computer.
Bubble Memory	A compact magnetic data storage system.
Buffer	A keyboard buffer is the area of the system used to store keystrokes without recording them on a disk. Data are stored in a printer buffer before they are printed.
Bullets	Large black dots placed in text to emphasize important content.
Byte	Eight bits, the number of bits usually used to store one character.
Centralized Loop	Devices containing magnetic loop tapes allowing more than one author to record text independently and/or simultaneously.
Character Set	Letters, numbers, punctuation marks, and symbols a printer is able to produce; typeface, pitch and symbols vary from one character set to another.
Chip	A tiny electronic device which uses integrated circuits to perform computer functions.
Command	Operator instruction that tells the system what to do.
Compatible	Equipment that can work together. For example, not all printers work with all computers. Computers are compatible if they can use the same software.
Continuous Forms	Connected paper forms that fold at perforated page boundaries eliminating the need to insert single pages.
Coupling	Two or more connected word processing systems permitting an exchange of information between the two.
CTRL	(Control key) - Key usually used within a command sequence. The CTRL key and another key are usually depressed at the same time to execute a specific command.
Cursor	Usually a rectangular or square flashing light or pulsating line indicating where the next keystroke will appear.
Daisy Wheel	A flat, plastic or metal print element with individual stems extending out from a circular disk; at the end of the stems are ''petals'' that contain individual letters, numbers, punctuation, etc.
Daisy Wheel Printer	A printer which uses a print wheel.

Database A collection of data necessary to carry on a business, or a unit of information that may be accessed by a computer.

Data Entry The process of putting information into a computer/information processor.

Debug To find and correct errors in a program.

Dedicated Line A communications channel between two locations used by a single operator or a single piece of equipment.

Discrete Media Magnetic tapes, disks, and other materials that can be removed from the recorder and delivered to the transcription center/individual.

Disk Drive A mechanism that holds a disk, retrieves information from the disk, and stores information on the disk.

Diskettes Flat, magnetic storage media with limited storage capacity available in 3 1/2, 5 1/4, and 8 inch diameters. Many are easily bent, hence the name "floppy disk."

Document Any piece of stored information that may be printed out on paper or displayed on the screen.

Dot Matrix A type of printer that uses a series of tiny dots to form characters.

Drive A device in a word processor/computer which is the location or address of a disk that has data stored on it. It may be referred to as Drive A, B, or C or the internal or external drive.

Drop Out The accidental loss of text from a document.

Elite The smaller of two character sizes used on typewriters and printers; also referred to as 12-pitch.

Execute To perform or carry out commands on a computer/word processor; usually by depressing the "return" key.

Extract To pick up items or information from another group of stored text.

Facsimile System A system used to transmit pictures, text, maps, etc., between geographically distant points.

File A collection of information stored on a disk, usually a document.

Floppy Disk A flexible magnetic storage medium on which files are stored.

Flowchart Diagram of a sequence of work operations to be carried out. Flowcharts also represent the sequence and logic of computer/word processing operations.

Flush Lines of text aligned either to the left margin (flush left) or to the right margin (flush right); the absence of indentations.

Folio Page number.

Footer Bottom margin of a document. If a footer includes any text, the text will appear on every page of the document.

Font Group of letters, numbers, symbols, etc. all in the same style; i.e., sans serif, modern, old English.

Format Layout of text in the final hard copy.

Form Feed Device on a printer that moves the paper forward as each line is finished.

Function Keys/Codes Specific keys or key combinations used to initiate operations such as deleting, inserting, and backspacing.

Global Search Capability to automatically search through stored data to find a certain word or group of words wherever it appears in the document.

Graphics Software capability for drawing charts, graphs, or pictures.

Hard Copy Document printed on paper.

Hard Disk Magnetic storage medium capable of permanently storing large amounts of information.

Hardware Physical equipment or components of a computer system.

Header Upper margin of a document and the text in that margin; usually includes the page number that will automatically be advanced on each new page.

Hot Zone Area at the right-hand margin.

Input Data entered into a computer or word processor.

Input/Output Technique, media, and devices used to achieve human/machine communication.

Interactive Word processors capable of communicating with computers or other word processors.

Interface Device that connects a word processor to a peripheral such as an OCR (Optical Character Recognition) scanner or a photocomposition machine.

Justify	To adjust lines of text so that each fits evenly between the left and right margins.
Memory	The area in the system which holds the instructions a processor/computer uses to accomplish requested tasks; also the area in which a document is held before it is stored.
Menu	List of operations from which the operator may chose.
Merge	To combine data from two or more separate files of information; frequently used in form letters to print the address and other variables in the text of the letter.
Mnemonic	Symbol, word, or device that helps the operator remember something; i.e., "c" for center, or "l" for line.
Network	Collection of processors and terminals that connects or serves more than one user at a time. The U.S. Postal Service uses a network to sort typed or printed mail.
Online	Refers to equipment in direct communication with the central processing unit of a computer.
Overprinting	Printing on top of other printing or beyond specified margins.
Pagination	Word processing function which divides a multi-page document into a desired or preset length or number of pages.
Peripherals	Any extra hardware and auxiliary storage units of a computer system.
Pica	The larger of two character sizes used on typewriters and printers; also referred to as 10-pitch.
Plotter	Device that produces graphics on a computer.
Program	Set of sequenced instructions that cause a computer to perform particular operations.
Purge	To remove unwanted data or information from a file.
Run Around	Arranging type around an illustration.
Queue	Series of stored documents waiting to be printed in order of storage.
QWERTY Keyboard	The name of the most common keyboard based on the first six letters on the third row. This keyboard was invented by Christopher Sholes in 1873.
Scroll	To move lines of text up or down on the display screen in order to view different parts of a document.

Sector Section on a disk that holds a specific number of characters.

Shared Logic Type of word processor in which several input/output devices and auxiliary storage equipment are handled by one central processing unit.

Software Set of programs, procedures, and routines used in the operation of a computer system.

Spreadsheet Program that uses a row and column arrangement of data to make calculations of that data.

Standalone Self-contained, single-unit having its own CPU, input/output terminal, and printer.

State Of The Art Expression used to describe the latest developments in a particular technical field.

Telecommunications Transmission of data over long distances via telephone, radio waves or satellite.

Terminal Any equipment on which data can be entered on a computer or transferred from a computer.

Text-editing Typewriter Typewriter that has the capability of storing, retrieving and editing through magnetic media.

Throughput Refers to the amount of information processing that can be accomplished in a given time.

Time Sharing System that allows many persons to use a word processor/computer at the same time.

Update To revise a document so that it contains the latest changes or information.

User-friendly Easy to use software and hardware.

Widow In printed text, a word or part of a line left standing by itself at the top of a page.

Word Originator Person originating a document.

Wording Memory Memory that stores and releases data.

Wraparound Automatic movement of the cursor downward to the next line as entries are typed; operator need not depress return key for line advance.

ACRONYMS from the WORLD of COMPUTERS

ADP	Automatic Data Processing
ALGOL	ALGOrithmic Language - a high-level computer language widely used in Europe.
BASIC	Beginners All-purpose Symbolic Instruction Code: a popular computer language.
BCD	Binary-Coded Decimal
CAD	Computer Aided Design
CAI	Computer Aided Instruction
CAM	Computer Aided Manufacturing
CAR	Computer Assisted Retrieval
COBOL	COmmon Business Oriented Language
CPS	Characters Per Second
CPU	Central Processing Unit - the brains of the computer. It controls the connecting computer units, holds the programs, and executes them.
CRT	Cathode Ray Tube - refers to the display screen
DOS	Disk Operating System
E-COM	Electronic Computer Originated Mail
INTELPOST	INTernational ELectronic POSTal Service
MC/ST	Magnetic Card Selectric Typewriter
MICR	Magnetic Ink Character Recognition - such as the bank code on the bottom of checks
MODEM	MOdulator-DEModulator. Device that converts electric signals into tones for transmission over telephone wires.
NCR	No Carbon Required. Chemically treated paper used instead of carbon paper to create copies.
OCR	Optical Character Reader. A scanner that reads printed or typed characters and converts them into signals for input into a data or word processor.
PBX	Private Branch EXchange. An in-house telephone network—also used to transmit data or text between other electronic equipment in the system.
RAM	Random Access Memory. Temporary memory of a computer/ word processor. Data disappears if machine is turned off.
ROM	Read Only Memory. Permanent memory of a computer/word processor.
UPC	Universal Product Code - Machine-readable code of parallel lines used for labeling much of today's packaged merchandise.
VDT	Video Display Terminal - display screen

Abbreviations

Abbreviations, words reduced to shorter forms, are acceptable in processing certain kinds of data. To eliminate confusion, however, only formally established and widely recognized abbreviations should be used. Listed here are some of the most commonly used in business.

a/c or acct.	account
adv. or advt.	advertisement
agcy.	agency
amt.	amount
a/p	accounts payable
approx.	approximately
appt.	appointment
a/r	accounts receivable
asst.	assistant
assn.	association
attn.	attention
atty.	attorney
B/S	balance sheet
B/B	bank balance
bf.	boldface
bd.	bond
B/L	bill of lading
B/P or B. pay.	bills payable
B/R or B. rec.	bills receivable
COD	cash on delivery
cc	courtesy copy
c. & f.	cost and freight
c. i. f. & c.	cost, insurance, freight, and commission

c/o	care of
chg.	charge
col.	column
con. or cont.	continued
corp.	corporation
cr.	credit
dept.	department
dir.	director
dstn.	destination
enc. or encl.	enclosure
e.e.	errors excepted
exec.	executive
ex.	example
fac. or FAX	facsimile
FX	foreign exchange
f.o.b.	free on board
fnd., fdg.	fund, funding
gen.	general
gds.	goods
guar.	guarantee
hdqrs.	headquarters
hr.	hour
I. C. & C.	invoice cost and charges
Inc.	incorporated
init.	initial
inst.	institute
inv.	invoice
invt.	inventory
JA	joint account
jour.	journal
jt.	joint
la. or lge.	large
leg.	legal
legis.	legislature, -tion
loc.	location
ltd.	limited
ltr.	letter
man.	manager, manual
mfg.	manufacturing
ms., MS ; mss, MSS	manuscript (s)
mkt.	market
mach.	machine
m.v.	market value

mdse.	merchandise
memo	memorandum
m.o.	money order
mtg.	mortgage; meeting
n.d.	no date
NA	not applicable/available
off.	office, officer
o.e.	omissions excepted
org.	organization
o.p.	out of print
o.t.	overtime
p., pp.	page (s)
pd.	paid
payt.	payment
pct.	percent
pfd.	preferred
prem.	premium
pres.	president
princ.	principal
ptg.	printing
pvt.	private
prod.	product
pub.	public, publication, -ing
qly.	quality
qty.	quantity
qtr.	quarter, -ly
ques.	question (s)
R.R.	railroad
Ry. , Rys.	railway (s)
re	in regard to
rcd.	received
rec.	receipt, record
Rec. Sec.	recording secretary
ref.	reference
reg.	regular, -ulation; register, -ed
retd.	returned
Rte., Rt.	route
sav.	saving (s)
sec., secy.	secretary
serv., svc.	service
sess.	session
/S/ or sgd.	signed
SOP	Standard Operating Procedure

synd.	syndicate
sys., systm,	system
tech.	technical
tel.	telephone, -graph, -gram
twp.	township
transp.	transportation
T.B.	trial balance
tr.	trust, trustee
unl.	unlimited, unlisted
ut.	utilities
val.	value, valuation
vs., v.	verse, versus
wrnt.	warrant
W/B ; WB	waybill, westbound
wt.	weight
w.i.	when issued
whsle.	wholesale
z., Z.	zone, zero, Zenith distance

ABBREVIATIONS USED IN LAW

ABA	American Bar Association
abstr.	abstract
ad val. (L. ad valorum)	according to value
admr.	administrator
admx.	administratrix
afft.	affidavit
crt.	circuit
D.A.	District Attorney
deb. rts.	debenture rights
D. C. L.	Doctor of Civil Law
D. Cn. L.	Doctor of Canon Law
D. J. S.	Doctor of Juridical Science
dkt.	docket
end.	endorse, -ed, -ment
exr., exec.	executor
exrx., execx.	executrix
J.	judge or justice
J. A.	Judge Advocate
J.A.G.	Judge Advocate General
J.D.	Doctor of Laws
JJ.	Justices
J.P.	Justice of the Peace
J.S.D.	Doctor of Juristic Sciences
J.U.D.	Doctor of both Canon and Civil law

L.	law
L. Ed.	Lawyer's Edition
leg.	legal
legis.	legislature, -tion
LL.B.	Bachelor of Laws
LL.D.	Doctor of Laws
L.S.	place of the seal
non seq.(L. non sequitur)	it does not follow
N.P.	Notary Public
ob.s.p. (L. obiit sine prole)	died without issue
P/A	Patent Office
P.P. (L. per procuratorem ____)	by proxy; on behalf of
p. & i.	protection and indemnity
P.L.	Public Law
prox. (L. proximo mense)	of the next month
ss or sc, scil. (L. scilicet)	namely; to wit
s.p. (L. sine prole)	without issue
TC	Tax Court

NOTE: Even though these are acceptable legal abbreviations, they should be used only when the originator of a legal document indicates. Do not use in general writing.

ABBREVIATIONS USED IN MEDICINE

AMA	American Medical Association
BMR	Basal metabolism rate
BUN	Blood urea nitrogen
CBC	Complete blood count
CVA	Cerebrovascular accident
D.C.	Doctor of Chiropractic
D.D.S	Doctor of Dental Surgery
D.D.Sc.	Doctor of Dental Science
D.O.	Doctor of Osteopathy
D & C	Dilation and Curettage
EEG	Electroencephalogram

EKG	Electrocardiogram
GI	Gastrointestinal
IU	Immunizing unit
IV	Intravenous
M.D.	Medical doctor
mg.	milligram
ml.	milliliter
mm.	millimeter
NAD	No apparent disease

NOTE: Abbreviation styles differ. The current trend is to omit periods in capital-letter abbreviations, except for doctors' academic degrees.

MEDICAL PREFIXES and SUFFIXES

Corresponding secretaries working in the medical industry will quickly learn prefixes and suffixes such as these:

arthro-	joint
cardio-	pertaining to the heart
cephal-	concerning the head or brain
dys-	ill, bad, not functioning well
-ectomy	a surgical removal
-gram	photograph of
-graphy	photographing
hyper-	increased; overactive
hypo-	beneath; decreased; underactive
-itis	inflammation
-ology	the study of
-otomy	cutting, but not removal; incision
path-, patho-	disease
-plasty	molding or formation as in plastic surgery
pyr-, pyret-	fever
ren-	refers to kidneys
tachy-	rapidly, as in abnormally rapid heart beat

STATE ABBREVIATIONS

Alabama (AL)
Alaska (AK)
Arizona (AZ)
Arkansas (AR)
California (CA)
Colorado (CO)
Connecticut (CT)
Delaware (DE)
District of Columbia (DC)
Florida (FL)
Georgia (GA)
Guam (GU)
Hawaii (HI)
Idaho (ID)
Illinois (IL)
Indiana (IN)
Iowa (IA)
Kansas (KS)
Kentucky (KY)
Louisiana (LA)
Maine (ME)
Maryland (MD)
Massachusetts (MA)
Michigan (MI)
Minnesota (MN)
Mississippi (MS)
Missouri (MO)
Montana (MT)
Nebraska (NE)
Nevada (NV)
New Hampshire (NH)
New Jersey (NJ)
New Mexico (NM)
New York (NY)
North Carolina (NC)
North Dakota (ND)
Ohio (OH)
Oklahoma (OK)
Oregon (OR)
Pennsylvania (PA)
Puerto Rico (PR)
Rhode Island (RI)
South Carolina (SC)
South Dakota (SD)
Tennessee (TN)
Texas (TX)
Utah (UT)
Vermont (VT)
Virgin Islands (VI)
Virginia (VA)
Washington (WA)
West Virginia (WV)
Wisconsin (WI)
Wyoming (WY)

FREQUENTLY USED ADDRESS ABBREVIATIONS

Assn	Association	Pl	Place
Blvd	Boulevard	Plz	Plaza
Expw	Expressway	Rdg	Ridge
Fwy	Freeway	Riv	River
Hts	Heights	R	Rural
Hwy	Highway	Shr	Shore
Hosp	Hospital	Sq	Square
Inst	Institute	Sta	Station
Jct	Junction	Ter	Terrace
Lk	Lake	Tpke	Turnpike
Mgr	Manager	Un	Union
Mdws	Meadows	Vw	View
Pky	Parkway	Vlg	Village

GEOGRAPHIC LOCATIONS

For sections of the country which are always capitalized, use the following abbreviation:

N	North	S	South	E	East
NE	Northeast	SE	Southeast	W	West
NW	Northwest	SW	Southwest		

APPENDIX C

Commonly Used Foreign Words and Expressions

There are certain French and Latin expressions that are commonly used in business communications. Be sure to check the correct spelling as well as pronunciation if you or your boss tend to use the following:

ad hoc	For this purpose only
aplomb	Self-assurance
avant-garde	Out in front, advanced
carte blanche	Unrestricted authority
cause celebre	Notorious event
coup d'etat	Sudden overthrow of government
esprit de corps	Group spirit
et al. (L.et alii)	And others
et cetera	And so on; and so forth
e.g. (L. exempli gratia)	For example
fait accompli	Accomplished fact
faux pas	Mistake
genre	Style or category
ibid, ib.	In the same place
i.e. (L. id est)	That is
ipso facto	By the fact itself
joie de vivre	Joy of living
laissez faire	Noninterference
motif	Theme; pattern
per annum	By the year
per diem	By the day
per capita	By the head
per se	By, of, or in itself

protege	One under the protection of another
pro tempore	For the time being
rendezvous	Meeting place; a meeting by appointment
R.S.V.P. or r.s.v.p. (Repondez s'il vous plait)	Please reply
sans	Without
savior faire	Experience; sophistication
status quo	Existing state of affairs
tete-a-tete	Private conversation between two persons
vice versa	The reverse

Special Signs and Symbols

The location of special signs and symbols on computer keyboards and word processors vary from one type of equipment to another. Some traditional typewriter keyboards do not offer some of these special characters; however, it is possible to create them by using combinations of other symbols and characters. Listed below are frequently used symbols in information processing.

— **DASH**	Strike two hyphens on either the typewriter or the computer keyboard to create this punctuation mark; leave no space before or after.
! **EXCLAMATION MARK**	The shift of the **1** key; space twice after it when it comes at the end of a sentence.
' **APOSTROPHE**	Use the apostrophe to represent feet in expressing measurements in feet and minutes in time; again do not space after the number before typing the symbol for feet or minutes.
" **QUOTATION MARK**	Use the quotation mark to represent measurements in inches and seconds in time; again, do not space after the number. Use the quotation mark to represent the ditto symbol; center the symbol under each word in line.
+ **PLUS SIGN**	Upper case on the = key on most keyboards; leave one space before and after. If your keyboard does not offer the plus, type a diagonal, backspace, and type a hyphen (/-).
x **MULTIPLICATION SIGN**	Use the small **x**; leave one space before and after.

-	**MINUS SIGN**	Use the hyphen key; leave one space before and after.
=	**EQUAL SIGN**	May be located on the number row or the third row; leave one space before and after.
÷	**DIVISION SIGN**	Division sign location varies; leave one space before and after. If there is no division sign on the typewriter, type a colon, backspace, type a hyphen.
~	**DIFFERENCE**	Leave one space before and after.
:	**RATIO: IS TO**	Use the colon for this symbol; leave one space before and after.
<	**LESS THAN**	Leave one space before and after.
>	**GREATER THAN**	Leave one space before and after.
^	**CARET**	Indicates an insertion.
()	**PARENTHESES**	Leave one space before and after the entire enclosure.
[]	**BRACKETS**	Used to enclose words inside parentheses or to indicate words changed inside quoted material. Leave one space before and after the entire enclosure. NOTE: Parentheses and brackets MUST be used in pairs.
°	**DEGREE SYMBOL**	If there is no degree symbol on your keyboard use the small o. No space after the number.
#	**NUMBER SYMBOL**	Used before a number to represent a number; used after a number to represent pounds; use no space between the number and the symbol in either case.
/	**DIAGONAL**	Virgule, solidus, separatrix, shilling, per—leave one space before and after the symbol; if typing a fraction leave no spaces before or after.
%	**PERCENT**	Leave no space between the number and the symbol.
®	**REGISTERED**	in the U.S. Patent Office
©	**COPYRIGHT**	
c/o	**CARE OF**	
@	**AT**	Leave one space before and after.
*	**ASTERISK**	Do not space when using an asterisk.

SPACE ONE—SPACE TWO

Word processors and computers are sensitive to correct spacing. In most cases, the rules learned in typing for spacing certain symbols and kinds of punctuation still apply.

- Always space twice after a colon (:) when you continue typing on the same line.

  I am taking four courses this quarter: history, math, music, and English.

- Always space one space after an abbreviation of a single word or initial.

  Mr. John A. Doe lives at 12 N. Elm Street.

- Always space once after a question mark within a sentence.

  Will there be two? three? or four? appointed?

- Always space once after a pair of parentheses.

  The new secretary has (1) excellent skills (2) common sense and (3) a pleasant personality.

- Leave no space within initial abbreviations.

  U.C.L.A. M.B.A. C.I.A.

- Leave no space before or after a hyphen except suspended hyphens in a series.

  She is a self-made woman.
  She showed us a 3-, 4-, and 5-bedroom house.

APPENDIX E

Travel Tips for the Secretary on the Go

Because of the expanded role of the secretary, secretaries today travel more than ever; and they are creating their own traveling style—LIGHT.

Here are tips for making packing easier and for staying well groomed on the trip.

- Carry three bags.
  - Small canvas or leather briefcase for business papers and small personal belongings.
  - Small bag for shirts or blouses, socks or hosiery, underwear and sleeping attire.
  - Hanging bag for suits, coats, jacket, dresses.

  All may be carried aboard a plane. Place the briefcase and small bag under the seat or in the overhead compartment.

  The flight attendant will hang the suitbag for you. This maneuver alone will save you a half-hour of your valuable time by not having to wait for your luggage to arrive.
- Carry a raincoat. The pockets are great for keeping small items handy. Also, it really might rain and nothing can ruin your appearance more than damp, wrinkled clothes. Hang the coat over your suitbag.
- Use your business address on luggage identification instead of your home address.
- Calculate in advance how to pack light.

Remember, you can get shaving cream or hair spray in Afghanistan.

- Check your wallet and key chain. Do you really need that Saks Fifth Avenue credit card or the key to your spouse's car? If you plan to shop on your trip, you will find that most major stores accept a major credit card. Take your American Express, and Mastercharge, or VISA card; leave the others behind.
- Emergency sewing kit. These are small and very handy. Not all hotels provide them.
- A chewable laxative. You can quickly adjust sleep patterns, but bodily functions are easily disrupted. It is important that you feel and act your best in representing your company.
- Treat yourself to a really good pen and keep it with you. In that way, you will be careful not to lose it. Cheap ones do not last and manage to disappear quickly.
- Travel in slacks and sports jacket or blazer. You can change later into a business suit for meetings. Women can switch the slacks for a coordinated skirt and stay with the same blouse and jacket. A wrinkled sports jacket does not look quite as bad as a wrinkled suit. If there is no time for a change, wear fabrics that do not wrinkle.

  NOTE: For those who travel extensively, keep a second set of toilet articles (comb, tooth brush and paste, shampoo, razor, etc.) packed at all times in your small canvas bag along with a folding umbrella and compact raincoat. You will always be ready to take off anywhere, anytime.
- If overseas travel seems likely, be sure you have a current passport. Apply for one at your nearest post office. Take along proof of citizenship and two passport photos to submit with the application. The post office takes about four weeks to process the application.

Otherwise, submit the application to a Passport Agency.

A Packing Technique to Avoid Wrinkling

- Suits: (1) Lay jacket on bottom of suitcase, sleeves flat pointing diagonally toward center of jacket below bottom button. (2) Place top half of trousers across top of jacket, flat and lined up on crease. (3) Fold bottom of jacket over top of trousers (or skirt). (4) Fold bottom of trousers or skirt across top of jacket. Criss-crossing provides extra cushioning.
- Shoes, shoe trees, other heavy objects: Pack along sides on bottom of suitcase to prevent clothes from shifting.
- Shirts and blouses: Remove laundry cardboard and stack. Alternate collars. Place each stack in a plastic bag to prevent shifting. Place over suits.
- Underwear: Fold in thirds and place in plastic bags over shirts. Do the same with lightweight sweaters, pajamas, gowns, handkerchiefs, scarves, etc.
- Socks, pantyhose, belts: Roll and place to fill spaces or shoes.
- Neckties: Fold neatly and place where no weight will crush them.
- Toilet kit: Place on top for easy access, or place in the small canvas bag.

Unpack upon arrival, even if you're staying only one night. To save time, hang wrinkled garments in the bathroom while you shower. The steam will remove the wrinkles.

APPENDIX F

Examples of Document Format

PUBLISHERS OF

1370 CHAIN BRIDGE ROAD · McLEAN, VIRGINIA 22101 · 703-356-3742

September 25, 19--

Ms. Super Sally Secretary, CPS
The XYZ Corporation
1234 Any Street
Your Town, XY 12345-6789

Dear Sally

Congratulations on being elected president of your Chapter of the Professional Secretaries International for the coming year. I read about this honor in the August issue of The Professional.

Secretaries happen to be very special to me; I have been a secretary as well as a teacher of secretarial subjects, and I write a monthly newsletter for secretaries. I am enclosing a couple of issues in case you have not seen it. In addition, I now have a book on the market called THE SECRETARY'S FRIEND.

Again, Sally, I congratulate you and wish you much success as the leader of such an outstanding organization.

Sincerely

Anne M. Morton, Editor/Author

ca

Enclosures

ADVERTISING · PUBLIC RELATIONS · PUBLISHING

Block, Open Punctuation

Stores
1370 Chain Bridge Rd
McLean, Virginia 22101
703-356-2525
304 Maple Avenue West
Vienna, Virginia 22180
703-255-2611

July 28, 19--

Mr. Peter Wang, Managing Director
Roe International Pte. Ltd.
Block 80, Kallang Bahru
#07-20/23
Singapore 1234

Dear Peter:

It seems that THE SECRETARY'S FRIEND newsletter is working for you, and we are glad. Enclosed is a copy of a letter from someone in your territory requesting information about the newsletter. Perhaps you will want to follow up on this.

We will have an exhibit at the National Office Products Association (NOPA) Show in Chicago in October. If you will be attending, I shall be looking forward to meeting you. I wish you continued success with THE SECRETARY'S FRIEND.

Sincerely,

Anne M. Morton, Editor

jj

Enclosure

Retailers
of
Fine Stationery
Writing Instruments
Office Supplies

Block, Mixed Punctuation

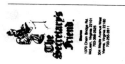

The Secretary's Friend.

Stores
1370 Chain Bridge Rd.
McLean, Virginia 22101
703-356-2525
304 Maple Avenue West
Vienna, Virginia 22180
703-255-2811

July 28, 19--

Mr. Peter Wang, Managing Director
Roe International Ltd.
Block 80, Kallang Bahru
Singapore 1234

Dear Peter:

It seems that THE SECRETARY'S FRIEND newsletter is working for you, and we are glad. Enclosed is a copy of a letter from someone in your territory requesting information about the newsletter. Perhaps you will want to follow up on this.

We will have an exhibit at the National Office Products Association (NOPA) Show in Chicago in October. If you will be attending, I shall be looking forward to seeing you. I wish you continued success with THE SECRETARY'S FRIEND.

Sincerely,

Anne M. Morton

Anne M. Morton, Editor

ca

Enclosure

Retailers of Fine Stationery Writing Instruments Office Supplies

Modified Block, Mixed Punctuation Indented Paragraphs

PUBLISHERS OF
The Secretary's Friend.
1370 CHAIN BRIDGE ROAD · McLEAN, VIRGINIA 22101 · 703-356-3742

September 25, 19--

Ms. Super Sally Secretary, CPS
The XYZ Corporation
1234 Any Street
Your Town, XY 12345-6789

Dear Sally

Congratulations on being elected president of your Chapter of the Professional Secretaries International for the coming year. I read about this honor in the August issue of The Professional.

Secretaries happen to be very special to me; I have been a secretary as well as a teacher of secretarial subjects, and I write a monthly newsletter for secretaries. I am enclosing a couple of issues in case you have not seen it. In addition, I now have a book on the market called THE SECRETARY'S FRIEND.

Again, Sally, I congratulate you and wish you much success as the leader of such an outstanding organization.

Sincerely

Anne M. Morton

Anne M. Morton, Editor/Author

ca

Enclosures

ADVERTISING · PUBLIC RELATIONS · PUBLISHING

Modified Block, Open Punctuation

PUBLISHERS OF

1370 CHAIN BRIDGE ROAD · McLEAN, VIRGINIA 22101 · 703-356-3742

December 9, 19--

Ms. Jane Smith, Supervisor
Word Processing Center
ABC Corporation
123 Any Street
Your Town, XY 12345-6789

AMS SIMPLIFIED LETTER

The Administrative Management Society (AMS) was originally referred to as the NOMA Simplified letter, because it was named from its founder, the National Office Management Association. When the organization changed its name to Administrative Management Society, of course, the letter name was also changed.

You will note a similarity in several ways to the Modern Simplified letter and to the style used in many government offices. The block style format with salutation and complimentary closing omitted is a timesaving feature of this letter style.

By triple spacing berfore and after the subject line and placing it in all capital letters, it makes the subject line immediately obvious to the reader for identifying the nature of the correspondence. The sender's name and title are also placed in all capital letters, four spaces after the last paragraph of the letter.

Please place this letter style as a sample in our company procedures manual to be used in the word processing center for all correspondence from the administrative offices. Thank you.

Anne M. Morton

ANNE M. MORTON, PRESIDENT

jj

ADVERTISING - PUBLIC RELATIONS - PUBLISHING

AMS Simplified

BUCK MORTON & ASSOCIATES 2 December 31, 19--

Since we have had so much success with your newsletter, we would like to stock your boo, THE SECRETARY'S FRIEND. Please provide us with further information. . . .

Style 2

BUCK MORTON & ASSOCIATES
Page 2
December 30, 19--

Since we have had so much success with your newsletter, we would like to stock your book, THE SECRETARY'S FRIEND. Please provides us with further information . . . .

Style 1

Second-Page Letter Headings

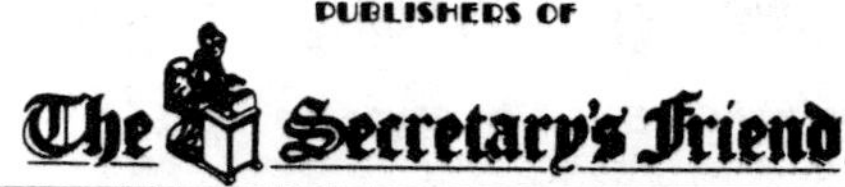

1370 CHAIN BRIDGE ROAD · McLEAN, VIRGINIA 22101 · 703-356-3742

25 September 19--

Ms. Sally Secretary, Supervisor
Word Processing Center
XYZ Corporation
1234 Any Street
Your Town, XY 12345-6789

MODERN SIMPLIFIED LETTER STYLE

Many executives, Sally, prefer a letter style referred to as "Modern Simplified." It is similar to the AMS (American Management Society) format with which many secretaries are already familiar. The block style with standard one-inch side margins for all letters is used as in memos.

As you will note above, military style is used for the date, followed by a triple space before and after the address. A subject line instead of a salutation is used, typed in all caps, with a triple space before and after it. There is no closing used in the letter, which is another timesaver. The wtiter's name and title are typed four lines below the body of the letter. The remainder of the letter parts are placed the same as for the traditional letter styles.

As a personal touch, it is suggested that the addressee's name be used in the beginning and in the ending paragraphs. This is really a nice touch to use for letters of any style.

If you prefer more information on letters, Sally, refer to BUSINESS LETTER TYPING, Second Edition, Casady and Casady, South-Western Publishing Company.

Anne M. Morton

Anne M. Morton, Editor

ca

ADVERTISING - PUBLIC RELATIONS - PUBLISHING

Modern Simplified Letter

PUBLISHERS OF

The Secretary's Friend.

1370 CHAIN BRIDGE ROAD · McLEAN, VIRGINIA 22101 · 703-356-3742

MEMORANDUM

TO: All Dealers

FROM: Anne M. Morton, Editor

DATE: September 25, 19--

SUBJECT: National Office Products Show

You are cordially invited to attend a reception at the Hyatt Regency, Downtown Chicago, on Friday evening, October 4, 7-9 p.m., to meet Tod J. Snodgrass, president, LOWEN PUBLISHING. Mr. Snodgrass will be available to answer any questions that you may have concerning his book, OFFICE PURCHASING GUIDE, as well as Lowen's latest title, THE SECRETARY'S FRIEND, and how these books can work for you.

jj

ADVERTISING - PUBLIC RELATIONS - PUBLISHING

Style 1 Heading

PUBLISHERS OF

The Secretary's Friend.

1370 CHAIN BRIDGE ROAD · McLEAN, VIRGINIA 22101 · 703-356-3742

MEMORANDUM

TO: All Dealers

FROM: Anne M. Morton, Editor

DATE: September 30, 19--

SUBJECT: National Office Products Show

You are cordially invited to attend a reception at the Hyatt Regency, Downtown Chicago, on Friday evening, October 4, 7-9 p.m., to meet Tod J. Snodgrass, president LOWEN PUBLISHING. Mr. Snodgrass will be available to answer any question that you may have concerning his book, OFFICE PURCHASING GUIDE, as well as LOWEN'S latest title, THE SECRETARY'S FRIEND, and how these books can work for you.

jj

ADVERTISING - PUBLIC RELATIONS - PUBLISHING

Style 2 Heading

Interoffice Memorandum Styles

PUBLISHERS OF

The Secretary's Friend.

1370 CHAIN BRIDGE ROAD · McLEAN, VIRGINIA 22101 · 703-356-3742

September 25, 19--

Contact Person: Carol J. Armstrong

Media Liaison

Phone: (123) 356-1970

FOR IMMEDIATE RELEASE

Suzy S. Kool, Administrative Assistant to the president, has been promoted to vice president in charge of management, XYZ Corporation. Ms. Kool has been with the company since graduating from the Morton Secretarial School. She also holds the office of secretary for the local chapter of Professional Secretaries International.

# # #

ADVERTISING - PUBLIC RELATIONS - PUBLISHING

Sample Press Release

PUBLISHERS OF

The Secretary's Friend.

1370 CHAIN BRIDGE ROAD · McLEAN, VIRGINIA 22101 · 703-356-3742

September 25, 19--

MEMORANDUM

TO: All Dealers

FR: Anne M. Morton, Editor

RE: National Office Products Show

You are cordially invited to attend a reception at the Hyatt Regency, Downtown Chicago, on Friday evening, October 4, 7-9 p.m., to meet Tod J. Snodgrass, president, LOWEN PUBLISHING. Mr. Snodgrass will be available to answer any questions that you may have concerning his book, OFFICE PURCHASING GUIDE, as well as Lowen's latest title, THE SECRETARY'S FRIEND, and how these books can work for you.

jj

ADVERTISING - PUBLIC RELATIONS - PUBLISHING

Style 3 Heading

APPENDIX G

Secretarial References

Secretarial Books and Manuals

Becker, Esther R., and Evelyn Anders. *The Successful Secretary's Handbook.* New York, NY: Harper & Row, Publishers.

Doris, Lillian, and Besse May Miller. *Complete Secretary's Handbook.* Englewood Cliffs, NJ: Prentice-Hall.

Engel, Pauline. *Executive Secretary's Handbook.* Englewood Cliffs, NJ: Prentice-Hall.

Flynn, Patricia. *The Complete Secretary.* Belmont, CA: Fearon-Pitman Publishers, Inc.

House, Sigler. *Reference Manual for Office Personnel,* 6th Edition. Cincinnati, OH: South-Western Publishing Co.

Hutchinson, Lois Irene. *Standard Handbook for Secretaries.* New York, NY: Gregg Division/McGraw-Hill Book Company.

Janis, J. Harold, and Margaret H. Thompson. *New Standard Reference for Secretaries and Administrative Assistants.* New York, NY: Macmillan, Inc.

Johnson, Mina M., and Norman F. Kallaus. *Records Management.* Cincinnati, OH: South-Western Publishing Co.

Kabbe, E. *Medical Secretary's Guide.* Englewood Cliffs, NJ: Prentice-Hall.

Kahn, Gilbert, Theodore Yerian, and Jeffrey R. Stewart, Jr., *Filing Systems and Records Management.* New York, NY: McGraw-Hill Book Co.

Miller, Besse May. *Legal Secretary's Complete Handbook.* Englewood Cliffs, NJ: Prentice-Hall.

Morton, Anne M. *The Secretary's Friend.* Torrance, CA: Lowen Publishing.

Sabin, William A. *Reference Manual for Stenographers and Typists.* New York, NY: Gregg Division/McGraw-Hill Book Co.

Taintor, Sarah, and Kate M. Monroe. *Secretary's Handbook.* New York, NY: Macmillan, Inc.

Whalen, Doris H. *The Secretary's Handbook.* New York, NY: Harcourt Brace Jovanovich, Inc.

Other Reference Sources

General

Information Please Almanac, Atlas, and Yearbook. New York, NY: Simon & Schuster, Inc.

Reader's Digest Almanac and Yearbook. New York, NY: W.W. Norton & Co., Inc.

Reader's Guide to Periodical Literature. New York, NY: The H. W. Wilson Company.

The World Almanac and Book of Facts. New York, NY: Doubleday & Co., Inc.

Dictionaries

The American College Dictionary. New York, NY: Random House, Inc.

The American Heritage Dictionary of the English Language. Boston, MA: American Heritage Publishing Co., Inc. and Houghton-Mifflin Company.

Funk & Wagnall's Standard College Dictionary. New York, NY: Harcourt Brace Jovanovich, Inc.

Roget's International Thesaurus of Words and Phrases. New York, NY: Crowell Collier and Macmillan, Inc.

Webster's New Collegiate Dictionary. Springfield, MA: G. & C. Merriam Company.

Webster's New World Dictionary of the American Language. New York, NY: World Publishing Co.

Specific Reference Sources

Address Abbreviations. Washington, D.C.: U.S. Postal Service Publication No. 59, U.S. Government Printing Office.

Bullinger's Postal and Shippers Guide for the United States, Canada, and New Foundland. Westwood, NJ: Bullinger's Guides, Inc.

Hotel and Motel Red Book. New York, NY: American Hotel Association Directory.

National ZIP Code Directory. Washington, D.C.: U.S. Government Printing Office.

Office Purchasing Guide. Snodgrass, Tod J. Torrance, CA: Lowen Publishing.

Official Airline Guide. Sausalito, CA: Official Airline Guide.

Rand McNally Commercial Atlas and Marketing Guide. Chicago, IL: Rand McNally & Company.

Grammar

Burtness, Paul S., and Alfred T. Clark, Jr. *Effective English for Business Communication.* Cincinnati, OH: South-Western Publishing Co.

Butera, Krause, and Sabin. *College English—Grammar and Style.* New York, NY: Gregg Division/McGraw-Hill Book Company.

Corbett, Edward. *The Little English Handbook.* New York, NY: John Wiley and Sons.

Frailey, L.E. *Handbook of Business Letters.* New York, NY: Prentice-Hall.

Hodges, John C., and Whitten, Mary E. *Harbrace College Handbook.* New York, NY: Harcourt Brace Jovanovich, Inc.

A Manual of Style. Chicago, IL: The University of Chicago Press.

Wolf, Morris P., Dale F. Keyser, and Robert R. Aurner. *Effective Communication in Business.* Cincinatti, OH: South-Western Publishing Co.

NOTE

Most of the above publications are available from your local bookstore or write for ordering information to:

Lowen Publishing
P.O. Box 6870-130
Torrance, CA 90504-0870

APPENDIX H

Proofreading Marks

Mark	Meaning	Example
⊏ ⊓ ⊐ ⊔	Reformat copy by moving copy in the direction of the brackets	⊏ In the beginning. . . (move left) (move right) ⊐ (move up) ⊓ (move down) ⊔
¶	Begin a new paragraph. Run paragraphs together	It is better this way. ¶ When it rains the river floods. no ¶ The damage can be heavy.
bf	Boldface type.	Side Heading bf
ital or ___	Underline or put in italics	Will you sink or swim? ital
℘	Delete copy.	It is not not necessary.
⁀	Close up horizontal space	Back ground is one word.
∧	Insert as indicated.	Pen paper, and folders are needed
#	Add a space.	Company, Inc.
lc	Use lower case	I love Summer fashions.
cap or ≡	Use capital letter.	Cap The face of fall is almost here.
DS SS	Space as indicated.	DS > Dear Committee Members Did you know. . .
‖	Align copy vertically.	‖ It is not. . . Although it was. . .
(sp)	Spell out the number or word.	I love (5th) (Ave) sp
stet	Ignore correction: let original stand.	Word processing is easy and fun. stet
=/	Insert hyphen.	The well known speaker
?	Not certain of meaning; question the writer.	The only thing constant about fashion is change. ?
sp?	Check spelling.	My secretary is my media liason sp
∼	Transpose words or letters.	I recieved the today package.

INDEX

A

Abbreviations, Business: Appendix B
Absence Of The Boss, Prepartion For: 78
Acronyms From The World Of Computers: 222
Adjusting To A New Boss: 142
And The Word Was Written: Chapter 7
And The Word Was Spoken: Chapter 8
Appointments, What To Do When They Run Behind: 126
Asking For A Pay Raise: 153

B

Business Abbreviations: 225
BUSINESS "BABBLE"—Do Not Let It Intimidate YOU!: Appendix A
Benefits, Fringe—How Many Are You Receiving?: 154
Business Reports, Processing: 108
Business Travel, Prepartion For: 76

C

Camera Skills, Acquiring: 131
Capital Vs. Lower Case—To Shift Or Not To Shift: 195
Changing Role Of The Secretary, The: Chapter 1
Coffee Break—Food For Thought: 57
Commonly Used Foreign Words And Expressions: Appendix C
Communication, Open (Office): 89
Computer Acronyms: 222
Computer Language And Terms Defined: 215
Computer Secrets, How to Keep Them: 56
Convention Planning: 69
Conversationalist, The Secretary As An Effective: 113
Copiers (Photo), Office Use: 38
Correspondence, Cost Cutting: 85
Correspondence, Answering Routine: 94
Criticism—You Can Handle It: 143

D

Decision Making: 50
Delegating Authority, The Art Of: 152
Direct Mail Terms: 164
Dictation, How To Give It Properly: 120
Diskettes, Security: 56
Document Formats: 243

E

Electronic Mail, Handling: 82
English Usage—Which Word (To Use) And Why: 204
Equipment, Selection Of: 33
Equipment, Placement Of: 34
Ergonomics In the Office: 35
Ethics, Office: 54
Examples Of Document Formats: Appendix F
Executive "Suite Talk": 148

F

File, Tickler: 29
Filing, Office: 40
Filing, Systems: 41
Filing, Micrographics: 43
Financial Reports, Preparing: 110
Flexitime: 52
Foreign Words And Expressions, Commonly Used: 233
Furniture, Selection Of: 33
Furniture, Placement Of: 34
Furniture, Ergonomics Of: 35

G

Gift Giving In The Office: 60
Grammatically Speaking: 198
Greeting The Office Visitor: 125

H

Handwriting In The Modern Office: 97
Holidays, Planning For: 58

I

Illness, When It Hits The Office: 149
Improving Your Reading Rate: 160
Information Sources And Resources: Chapter 11
IRS, Prepartion For: 74

J

Job Sharing: 52

K

Keeping Information Confidential: 55
Keeping The Lines Of Communication Open: Chapter 6
Keyboard, Dvorak: 175

L

Letter Closings, Which To Use: 102
Letter Formats, Choosing An Economic One: 104
Listening, An Important Secretarial Skill: 90
Logging Work Increases/Productivity: 63

M

Mail (Electronic), Handling: 82
Mail (Office), Handling: 80
Mailing Lists, Learning To Work With: 163
Mailing Terms: 164
Media, The Secretary Deals With The: 128
Meeting Types: 64
Meetings, Prepartion For: 65
Metric. . .When?: 172
Minutes, Taking Them At A Meeting: 67

N

Negative Approach Isn't All Bad, The: 146
Newsletters—A Growing Pool Of Information: 161
NOPA: National Office Products Association: 133

O

Office As A Community, The: Chapter 4
Office As A Production Unit, The: Chapter 5
Office Design/Planning/Layout: 33
Office Ethics: 54
Office Mail, Handling: 80
Office Politics, How To Handle It: 147
Office, Relocation: 45
Office Space And Equipment, The: Chapter 3
Outside World, The: Chapter 9

P

Passing The Hat: 60
Pay Raise, How To Ask For A: 153
Photocopiers, Office Use: 38
Photographic Skills, Acquiring: 131
Planning And Attending Meetings: 64
Planning The Business Trip: 76
Post Office Procedures: 166
Post Office Services: 169
Poor Paragraphing, How To Correct: 100
Preparation For Meetings: 65
Press Releases, Preparing: 130
Procedures Manuals: 61
Processing Business Reports: 108
Productivity, Secretary's Responsibility For: 61
Professional Reading: 159
Proofreading: 111
PSI (Professional Secretaries International): 177
Public Relations Liaison, The Secretary As: 128
Punctuation And Mechanics: 183

Q

Quick And Easy Brush-up—Spelling, Punctuation, Grammar: Chapter 12

R

Reference Sources For The Office: 159
References, Secretarial: 247
Routine Correspondence, The Secretary Answers: 94

S

Salutations, Which To Use: 101
Secretaries: The Human Element In Office Systems: 137
Secretary And Boss—A Winning Team: 141
Secretary, As Supervisor: 49
Secretary—The Good-will Ambassador: 125
Secretary, Changing Role: 23
Secretary, Other Job Titles: 25
Secretary, Preparation For First Job: 27
Secretary Speaks, The: 113
Secretarial References: Appendix G
Secretarial Tips And Timesavers: Chapter 13
Secretarial Writing Skills: 93
Security, Diskettes: 57
Sex Bias In Writing, How To Eliminate It: 103
Shorthand, Brushing Up: 97
Special Signs And Symbols: Appendix D
Speech Preparation Techniques: 114
Spelling—The Sandtrap Of The Secretary: 179
Staff Confidante, The Secretaries Role As: 139
Stress—Learning To Cope: 144
''Suite Talk''—Translating Executive Conversation: 148

T

Tax Audit, Secretary's Prepartion For: 74
Taking Minutes At A Meeting: 67
Teleconferencing: 73
Telecommuting: 52
Terminals, Video Display: 38
Telephone Personality—Create It: 116
Travel Tips For The Secretary On The Go: Appendix E
Two-Martini Lunch Crowd, The Secretary Deals With The: 151

U

Unscrupulous Callers, Handling: 133
U.S. Postal Service—A Cost-Effective Friend: 166

V

VDTs (Video Display Terminials): 38

W

Within The Office Environment: Chapter 10
Work Area, Efficiency: 43

Y

Your First Job As A Secretary: Chapter 2

FREE Updates
FREE Office Success Catalog

Important Information For All Office Professionals

n this fast-moving world of ours, things are constantly changing. To help ı keep up, here are two **FREE** offers:

• **FREE** Update. Mail in this coupon and we'll rush you out the latest ɔrmation-updates on the subjects covered in this book.

• **FREE** Catalog. If the information and ideas in this book have been nulating and helpful to you, we're confident you'll also enjoy the other pub- ations carried by Lowen Publishing. If you'd like to receive a **FREE** copy our Office Success Catalog, please fill out and return this coupon.

YES, send me a **FREE** copy of the latest updates on this book.

YES, send me a **FREE** copy of your Office Success Catalog.

r Name ______________________ Title ____________

npany Name ______________________ Date ____________

eet Address ______________________________

/, State, Zip ______________________________

ne No. (______) ______________________________

nature ______________________________

ɔroximate number of employees in your office ____________

Send to:

Lowen Publishing / P.O. Box 6870-130 / Torrance, CA 90504 / (213) 831-2770

Office Succ

WRITE RIGHT! is an invaluable tool for executives, secretaries, students . . . it illustrates the right and wrong ways (to write) by easy-to-grasp examples.
—Los Angeles Times

A Desk Drawer Digest of Punctuation, Grammar & Style, **WRITE RIGHT!** is an easy-to-use reference, that covers all the essentials. Venolia uses lively quotations to illustrate rules, making information easy to understand and remember.

WRITE RIGHT! paperback, 126 pages

A treasury of literacy, full of good advice about writing of all kinds. *—Los Angeles Times*

BETTER LETTERS: A Handbook of Business & Personal Correspondence. This well-written book brings the art of letter writing up to date. It provides sample letters that cover everything from job applications to letters of resignation, from complaints to thank-you notes.

BETTER LETTERS paperback, 172 pages.

These two books by Jan Venolia are sold as a two-book

The **Standard Forms Book** contains virtually every form you'll ever need to efficiently run an office. Each form is a full 8½'' x 11'' size and they even include room for your company logo and address. All forms are printed on heavy stock paper and perforate easily out of the book. Reusable time and time again, the forms include accounting, purchasing, sales, operations, shipping, maps, graphic aids and more. Copy on your photocopier or have them printed.

Standard Forms Book, contains 248 forms
Item No. FBS-2 softcover **$14.95**

The **Deluxe Forms Book** contains virtually every form you'll ever need to efficiently run an office. Each form is a full 8½'' x 11'' size and they even include room for your company logo and address. All forms are printed on heavy stock paper and perforate easily out of the book. Reusable time and time again, the forms include accounting, purchasing, sales, operations, shipping, maps, graphic aids and more. Copy on your photocopier or have them printed.

Deluxe Forms Book, contains over 400 forms
Item No. FDB-1 softcover **$29.95**

A ''must have'' for any office that deals with printers.
—Graphics Journal

Inclusiveness and fine illustrations are this book's major strengths. It is technical yet accessible, instructional but interesting.
—Library Journal

The indispensable reference book for everyone who plans, designs, or buys printing. Chapters lead you from planning your printing through typesetting, camera ready copy, photographs, preparation and proofs, offset printing, other printing methods, to bindery. Fifty technical illustrations, 500-word glossary. 4-Color photos.

Getting it Printed: How To Work with Printers and Graphic Arts Services to Assure Quality, Stay on Schedule, and Control Costs. 248 pages.

Item No. 8-8 hardcover **$42.50**
Item No. 7-X softcover **$29.50**

This is not just another resume book. It is instead thorough and understandable. It's loaded with practical examples and covers specific populations, i.e. career changers, re-entry people (back-into-the-labor-market) and other paper work that should accompany a resume (cover letter, marketing letters.)

The book gives the job seeker interview and negotiating tips, telephone techniques, and more:
—one resume example is presented in seven different formats.
—there's an excellent suggestion—with examples—of having the job seeker prepare a detailed sketch of all former employment situations.

Resume Power: Selling Yourself On Paper
by Tom Washington, 288 pages

Publications

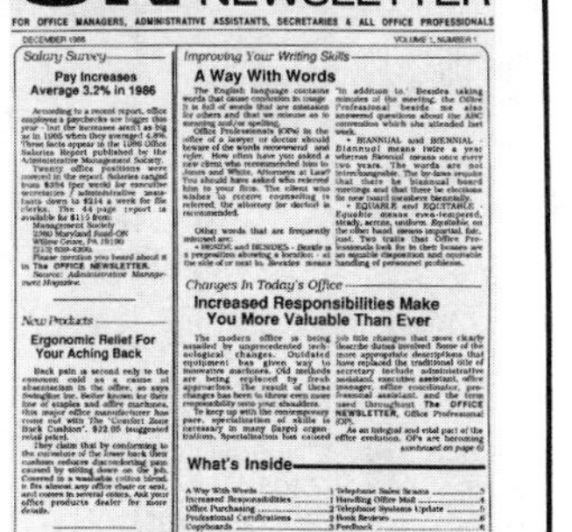

The **OFFICE NEWSLETTER (ON)** is written to help all Office Professionals do their job better, and easier. Each issue of **ON** is enjoyable, easy-to-read, and is jam-packed with ideas to help boost production, save valuable time and money, and keep you up to date on such topics as Communications, Compensation, New Products, Office Purchasing, Personal Money-Saving Tips, Helpful Office Hints, and much, much more.

DISTINGUISHED EDITORS

The articles that appear in **ON** are created and written monthly by a knowledgeable group of contributing editors: those who work in offices and those who instruct Office Professionals.

SUPER BONUS

Order a 1 year subscription NOW and Save One-Half! That's right, subscribe to **ON** right away and you'll receive a 50% Charter Subscriber discount! Instead of the normal $96, you'll pay only $48 for a full 12-month subscription. Or try a 6-month trial subscription for just $36.

The **OFFICE NEWSLETTER**

Item No. ON 12 (1 year) **$48**
Item No. ON 6 (6 months) **$36**
Item No. ON 1 (Sample Copy) .... **$ 1**

A **highly recommended** and valuable reference source for all office professionals. . . an excellent book.
— National Business Education Association, Anne Matthews, President

An excellent resource publication for every office.
—Senator John Warner

This book is a primer for both the experienced and the novice in the office world, offering a wide range of topics from Office Design and Planning, to How to Ask for a Raise, to Being a Good Conversationalist. **The Secretary's Friend's** pages are filled with useful, easy to read information on how to better manage, communicate with and handle people.

The Secretary's Friend: The Office Management Manual by Anne Morton, 256 pages

Item No. 16-6 hardcover **$14.95**
Item No. 33-6 softcover .... **$ 9.95**

Snodgrass' book can mean big savings and thus larger profits for any company.
—Dallas Morning News

Snodgrass' easy-to-read book is loaded with reliable information.
—The Office Professional Newsletter

A guide to making good purchasing judgments. Thorough. The subjects are covered very well.
—Library Journal

Office Purchasing Guide is a *MUST* for every office. This easy-to-read manual is very valuable. Whether you're buying clips or computers, pens or printing, it will make your job less difficult. Written by an expert in the field, it clears up the confusion that often goes along with the job of buying for the office.

Office Purchasing Guide: How to Buy Better, Easier and Save up to 50% on Office Supplies & Furniture, Business Forms & Printing, Office Machines & Equipment. By Tod Snodgrass, 256 pages

Item No. 02-6 hardcover **$19.95**
Item No. 15-8 softcover **$14.95**

PLEASE COMPLETE THE ORDER FORM BELOW AND MAIL IT IN

Qty.	Item No.	Title	Price Each Dollars	Price Each Cents	Total Price Dollars	Total Price Cen

(Attach separate sheet for additional selections)

Subtotal ________

CA Res. add 6½% Sales Tax ________

Shipping $3.00 for first book $1.50 for each additional book
(No postage & handling on subscriptions) ________

THANK YOU FOR YOUR ORDER — TOTAL AMOUNT ________

Our Guarantee

All products have our standard money-back guarantee. If for any reason you are ever dissatisfied with any purchase from Lowen Publishing, just return it (in good sellable condition) for a full refund. Subscription refunds are for the unmailed copies.

MAIL TO: Lowen Publishing
P.O. Box 6870-130
Torrance, CA 90504
(213) 831-2770

Your Name ________ Title ________

Company Name ________

Street Address ________

City, State, Zip ________

Daytime Phone No. (   ) ________

Signature ________ Date ________

Check One: ☐ Check Enclosed ☐ Bill My Company (No CODs)

Ck# ________ P.O.# ________ (Option

All orders to be billed must contain a company, library, school or government street address to be processed. No post offi box numbers please. Personal orders must be accompanied by payment.